California
Government
and Politics
Today

California Government and Politics Today

Eighth Edition

Mona Field
Glendale Community College

Charles P. Sohner
El Camino College, Emeritus

 LONGMAN

An Imprint of Addison Wesley Longman, Inc.

New York • Reading, Massachusetts • Menlo Park, California • Harlow, England
Don Mills, Ontario • Sydney • Mexico City • Madrid • Amsterdam

Executive Editor: Pam Gordon
Acquisitions Editor: Peter Glovin
Project Manager: Ellen MacElree
Design Manager: Wendy Fredericks
Cover Design: Kay Petronio
Cover Photograph: Digital Stock
Art Studio: ElectraGraphics, Inc.
Prepress Services Specialist: Valerie Vargas
Electronic Production Specialist: Joanne Del Ben
Electronic Page Makeup: Joanne Del Ben
Printer and Binder: Maple-Vail Book Manufacturing Group
Cover Printer: Coral Graphic Services, Inc.

Library of Congress Cataloging-in Publication Data

Field, Mona.
    California government and politics today / Mona Field, Charles P.
Sohner.—8th ed.
      p.   cm.
    Includes bibliographical references and index.
    ISBN 0-321-00511-2
    1. California—Politics and government—1951-   I. Sohner, Charles
P. II. Title.
JK8716.F54 1998
360.9794—dc21   98-27311
                                                     CIP

ISBN 0-321-00511-2

1 2 3 4 5 6 7 8 9 10—MA—98992020

Contents

Preface

Since the time of earliest explorers and conquistadores, California has held a mystique of golden potential for people from all over the world. Today's California is a reflection of its own past as well as a complex, ever-changing mosaic of the future. It is a destination for many, even as others are choosing to leave. California today is a "salad bowl" of ethnicities, classes, and cultures, all of whom must coexist despite their many differences.

It is this text's goal to present the complexity not only of the political process but also of the social and economic circumstances in California today. The concise (yet thorough) exploration of these themes is designed to give readers many opportunities to reflect on their experiences living here and to consider ways in which they can become part of the process.

A number of features make the text accessible to readers: opening quotations for each chapter; charts and maps; and appendixes, including a glossary defining each word that appears in italics in the text, a list of useful addresses on the World Wide Web, and a list of political organizations accessible to students. In addition, each chapter closes with "Questions to Consider," designed to help readers evaluate the material through their own personal reflections and critical thinking.

Special emphases of this edition that add to its currency are the issues relating to numerous ballot initiatives the courts are evaluating, the long-awaited turnaround in the state's economy, the continuing increases in population and in social and cultural diversity, and the expansion of the electorate to include new citizens eager to vote. As always, the book pays close attention to demographic and economic indicators and their political implications.

Supplements

Instructor's Manual/Test Bank. Written by Mona Field, this resource includes test questions as well as a brief study guide for students that instructors can copy and distribute. The study guide can also be downloaded through the Longman Web site at http://longman.awl.com. To access the study guide from the home page, click on "search our catalog," type "Field" in the author section, and choose *California Government and Politics Today*, Eighth Edition. The study guide will be available through the product information sheet for the book.

Acknowledgments

The authors' highest aim is to enlighten and inform the readers while gently reminding them that the fate of our Golden State is in our hands. If we do not participate, who will? We hope our efforts are successful, and we are grateful to those who made this book possible. We thank our editor, Peter Glovin. We would also like to recognize the contributions of our reviewers: Lyndelle Fairlie, San Diego State University; Gerald R. Farrington, Fresno City College; David Meneffee-Libey, Pomona College; Stanislav Perkner, Humphreys College; and Ron Schmidt, California State University, Long Beach. Finally, of course, we thank our families, who understand our periodic disappearances into our offices.

We remain fully responsible for our work, both the positive aspects and any omissions or errors it may contain.

Please read, reflect, and consider joining us in a long-term commitment to make California the very best it can be.

MONA FIELD
CHARLES P. SOHNER

California
Government
and Politics
Today

California Politics in Perspective

The goose is laying her golden eggs again.

—*Forbes*

After a rocky start to the decade, Californians seem to be approaching the close of the century with a renewed sense of satisfaction and hope. The economy has emerged from a long, painful recession that began when the Cold War ended. Today's California is booming with new or revived industries, including high technology, biomedical research, entertainment, telecommunications, and tourism. The state is still number one in the country in agricultural production[1] and boasts the nation's two busiest ports (Long Beach and San Pedro) in terms of export-import traffic.[2] If California were a separate nation, it would rank eighth in the world in its gross domestic production.

In addition to the booming economy, California still leads the nation in population, with hints that by the year 2010 the state will be home to about 37 million Americans, of whom more than half will be "minorities." California's influence on the national scene will continue to be enormous, and individual Californians with the right education and skills will continue to do very well. Some of the *scapegoating* and *polarization* of the early 1990s may have run their course, leaving room for a more inclusive, generous approach—now that the economy is better, tax revenues are higher, thus allowing politicians to spend more money on essential public services or to cut taxes, depending on which path California voters support. As the good news of California's economic recovery spreads, even some of the "refugees" who left the state during the early 1990s are returning to California, having realized that the grass was not greener in Montana, Oregon, or Arizona.[3]

Yet despite the overall strength of the economy and the related improvements in public services, California still remains a *two-tier* state in which those without adequate education remain caught in low-wage, no-benefits jobs or have no jobs at all. The state's public schools rank 47th

1

in the nation in terms of textbook spending,[4] while personal bankruptcy filings are at record levels in part due to underemployment.[5] California is still a land of extremes between rich and poor, and the governor who will lead the state into the next century will have to guide California toward increased opportunities for everyone yet preserve some form of public support for those who have not yet achieved the "California dream."

National Impact: Setting Trends for the Country

In the year 2000, California celebrates its sesquicentennial (150th anniversary of statehood) as perhaps the most powerful state in the nation. Because national political power is directly linked to population, and because California has remained the most populous state for several decades, California maintains its enormous clout in the national scene. Two of the last six presidents, Richard Nixon and Ronald Reagan, came from California, and of the nine justices currently on the U.S. Supreme Court, four were either born or educated in California. The state has 52 of the 435 members of the House of Representatives, 11 more than any other state, and 54 *electoral votes*, one-fifth of the 270 necessary to elect a president.

California's national importance flows largely from three traditional sources of political power—money, publicity, and population. Even during the prolonged economic slump of the early 1990s, California remained the home of one-fifth of the nation's wealthiest people.[6] Although the rich are a tiny minority of the population, they can have enormous influence on politics, both through campaign contributions and through their own political activism. The emerging custom of wealthy individuals using their own money to run for office resulted in the election of Richard Riordan as mayor of Los Angeles and fueled the *gubernatorial* race of Al Checchi.

Along with dollars, media and publicity also play a key role in political outcomes. During both good times and bad, California gets an ample share of attention in the national media. The state still gets international media coverage for happy events such as the annual Tournament of Roses Parade as well as less favorable attention when its residents suffer the ravages of earthquakes or major fires. Because California is home to people from all over the world, events in Los Angeles or San Francisco may be front-page news in Manila, Ho Chi Minh City, Seoul, Hong Kong, or San Salvador.

It is sheer numbers, however, that contribute most to California's political might. Table 1.1 shows how the population has grown. California's 32.5 million people[7] earn the state both the largest congressional delegation and the largest bloc of electoral votes and also, under most circumstances, enable it to receive more federal grants and government contracts than almost any other state. It is no surprise that presidential candidates often visit California more times than any other state as they campaign for those electoral votes, and it is no wonder that high-level California politicians are often mentioned as future presidential contenders.

Table 1.1

California's Population: Growth Since Statehood

Year	Population
1850	92,597
1860	379,994
1870	560,247
1880	864,694
1890	1,213,398
1900	1,485,053
1910	2,377,549
1920	3,426,861
1930	5,677,251
1940	6,907,387
1950	10,586,223
1960	15,717,204
1970	19,971,069
1980	23,667,902
1990	31,400,000
1997	32,609,000
projected 2005	38,200,000

Source: U.S. Census Bureau, State Department of Finance.

The State and Its People: Power Blocs in Conflict

Despite California's prominence in national affairs, the daily lives of its people are affected more closely by the politics of their own state. The state determines the grounds for divorce, the traffic regulations, public college tuition fees, penalties for drug possession, and the qualifications one needs to become a barber, psychologist, or lawyer. It establishes the amount of unemployment compensation, the location of highways, the subjects to be taught in school, and the rates to be charged by telephone and gas and electric companies. Along with the local governments under its control, it regulates building construction, provides police and fire protection, and spends about 15 percent of the total value of goods and services produced by California residents.

The policy decisions made in these and other areas are influenced by the distribution of political power among various groups with competing needs and aspirations. Some of the power blocs reflect the same conflicts of interest that the nation experiences: labor versus business, landlords versus tenants, environmentalists versus oil companies. But, as in so many things, these battles are fought on a grander scale in California. With its incredibly complex array of local governments, including over 6,000 *special districts* to provide everything from street lights to public education, California's political system almost defies understanding. No wonder that voters have shown their overall mistrust of elected officials and turned to *ballot initiatives* to make new laws and even to amend the state constitution.

These ballot initiatives, or *propositions*, deal with everything from medical use of marijuana to patients' rights, from "three strikes and you're out" to affirmative action. While political experts bemoan the use of initiatives to set public policy, the voters keep signing petitions to place these items on the ballot. The outcome of these initiative battles usually depends on such factors as money, media, and the public mood.

The State and the Federal System: A Complex Relationship

Like the other states, California is part of the American federal system. *Federalism* distributes power to both the national and state governments, thereby creating a system of dual citizenship and authority. It is a complex arrangement designed to assure the unity of the country while at the same time permitting the states to reflect the diversity of their people and economies. Although national and state authority overlap in such areas as taxation and highway construction (examples of what are known as concurrent powers), each level of government also has its own policy domain. The U.S. Constitution gives the national government its powers, including such areas as interstate commerce, foreign policy, national defense, and international relations. The states are permitted to do anything that is not prohibited or that the Constitution does not assign to the national government.

Within each state, the distribution of powers is *unitary*. This means that the cities, counties, and other units of local government get their authority from the state. States and their local bodies generally focus their powers on such services as education, public safety, and health and welfare.

Just as California has a mighty impact on the country as a whole, the national government exerts reciprocal influence on the states. Federal funds often come with strings attached. The federal welfare reform statutes of 1996 created demanding new requirements for every state that wanted to continue to get federal funds for welfare recipients. California's elected officials were forced to create innovative programs and new limitations on public assistance in order to meet federal regulations. Such federal *mandates* continue to cause debate over *states' rights* and the proper role of the federal government, with recent trends suggesting that *devolution*, or the passing of authority from federal to state and local governments, will continue.

However, federal funds do not always come directly to government itself. For nearly fifty years, between World War II and the end of the Cold War, California's private defense industry relied heavily on federal contracts to create a thriving military-based economy. Major corporations, such as Lockheed, Hughes, Rockwell, and many others, enjoyed high profits and provided well-paying, secure jobs to engineers, managers, secretaries, and assembly-line workers. When the Cold War ended in 1989, this entire military contract system crashed abruptly, leaving a large hole in the California economy. The layoffs and their ripple effects into the affected communities have continued throughout the decade, creating both economic and emotional stress for tens of thousands of individuals. Fortunately, in recent years, the economies of areas hit hard by *demilitarization* have found new ways to grow. San Diego's "Wireless Valley," Southern California's South Bay emphasis on international trade and San Francisco's Presidio Park are good examples of creative responses to the loss of military dollars. Retraining, education, and job creation continue to be themes for California as it recovers from its longtime dependence on the federal defense budget.

While relations between the federal government and each state are complex and significant, the relations between states are also important. The U.S. Constitution requires every state to honor the laws of every other state, so that marriages and other contracts made in one state are respected in all states and criminals trying to escape justice cannot find safe haven by leaving the state in which they have been convicted.

Federalism is perhaps America's greatest political invention. It permits states to enact their diverse policy preferences into law on such matters as gambling, prostitution, trash disposal, and wilderness protection, and thus encourages experiments that may spread to other states. California has become known as a place of experimentation, and new political ideas from this state often spread across the nation. Conservative themes such as tax revolts, anti-immigration sentiments, and the backlash against affirmative action all began as successful ballot propositions in California, while liberal ideas such as legalization of marijuana for medical purposes and legal protections for gays and lesbians also began here.

Because federalism allows states great autonomy, and because California has developed a complex web of local governments, the average California voter must make numerous decisions at the ballot box. Each Californian, whether a citizen or not, lives in a number of election jurisdictions, including a congressional district, a state Senate district, an Assembly district, and a county supervisorial district, plus (in most cases) a city, a school district, and a community college district (Figure 1.1 lists officials elected by voters). This array of political jurisdictions provides many opportunities to exercise democracy. It also creates confusion, overlaps, and many occasions on which voters feel unable to fully evaluate the qualifications of candidates or the merits of ballot propositions.

Other problems linked to federalism include outdated state boundaries that have created some "superstates," with land masses and populations that may be ungovernable, and the differences in resources between states. California's size has certainly caused numerous controversies over whether the state should be divided somehow. Meanwhile, variations in states' resources perpetuate inequality in schools, public hospitals, and

Partisan Offices			
National Level	**Elected by**	**Term**	**Election Year**
President	Entire state	4 years	Years divisible by four
U.S. Senators	Entire state	6 years	Every six years counting from 1992
			Every six years counting from 1994
Members of Congress	Districts	2 years	Even-numbered years
State Level			
Governor[1]			
Lt. Governor[1]			
Secretary of State[1]	Entire state	4 years	Even-numbered years when there is no presidential election
Controller[1]			
Treasurer[1]			
Attorney General[1]			
Insurance Commissioner			
Members of Board of Equalization[1]	Districts	4 years	Same as governor
State Senators[1]	Districts	4 years	Same as governor for even-numbered districts
			Same as president for odd-numbered districts
Assembly members[2]	Districts	2 years	Even-numbered years

Nonpartisan Offices			
State Level			
Superintendent of Public Instruction	Entire state	4 years	Same as governor
Supreme Court justices	Entire state	12 years	Same as governor
Court of Appeal justices	Entire state	12 years	Same as governor
Superior Court judges	Counties	6 years	Even-numbered years

[1]Limited to two terms by Proposition 140
[2]Limited to three terms by Proposition 140

Figure 1.1   Federal and State Officials Elected by California Voters.

Source: League of Women Voters.

other government facilities at a time when the nation as a whole is concerned about how to provide these services. The federal system also promotes rivalry between states as they compete to attract new businesses (and jobs) or keep existing ones. Among the tactics used in this struggle are tax breaks, reduced worker compensation, and relaxed environmental protection standards. Nevada, with its lower taxes, attracts some California enterprises, while Utah offers a highly educated workforce and relatively low crime rates as primary incentives for businesses to relocate. On a larger and more complex scale, the appeal of relocating across the border in Mexico has been enhanced by the passage of the North American Free Trade Agreement (NAFTA), which eliminates import tariffs and encourages American companies to open factories where wages are low and worker protection is minimal. In the global economy of the new millennium, California faces tremendous challenges in providing decent jobs, education, health services, and, in general, the high quality of life that the state has always promoted as its chief claim to fame.

Questions to Consider
Using Your Text and Your Own Experiences

1. What are some of the pros and cons of life in California? Do these depend in part on whether you live in a rural or urban area?

2. What are some of the challenges facing the state as it enters the new millennium? What can elected officials do to resolve these challenges? How do you fit into the challenges facing our state?

3. Take a class survey. How many students were born in California? How many are immigrants, either from another state or another nation? Team up so that an "immigrant" is paired with a "native" Californian. Teams or pairs can discuss the different experiences of those born here versus those who immigrated.

Notes

1. Dave Lesher, "Officials Crow About State's Farm Economy," *Los Angeles Times,* 17 July 1997, p. A3.
2. Tim W. Ferguson, "California's Comeback," *Forbes,* 20 November 1995, p. 141.
3. Lisa Taylor, "We're Ba-aack!" *Los Angeles Times,* 30 March 1997, p. K1.
4. U.S. Department of Education, Association of American Publishers, as cited in "In a Book Bind," *Los Angeles Times,* 28 July 1997, p. A1.
5. Patrice Apodaca and Don Lee, "Personal Bankruptcies Climbed in State," *Los Angeles Times,* 11 February 1997, p. D2.
6. "Bill Gates Tops List in Forbes Ranking of Richest in U.S.," *Los Angeles Times,* 3 October 1994, p. D1.
7. Robert A. Rosenblatt, "Strong Growth Projected for California," *Los Angeles Times,* 29 January 1997, p. D2.

Chapter 2

The Californians: Land, People, and Political Culture

There will always be a California dream . . . but it won't come with mere wishing. . . . We must all become "dreamers of the day," exploring the future with eyes and hearts wide open.

—A. G. Block, journalist

The political process in California, as in other states, is conditioned by many geographic, *demographic,* and cultural influences. While geography changes only slowly, population shifts and cultural influences can rather suddenly inject new and unpredictable threads into the complex web that forms the state's identity and future prospects.

Geographic Influences: Where Are We?

With an area of 156,000 square miles, California is larger than Italy, Japan, or England and is the third-largest state, following Alaska and Texas. It is shaped like a gigantic stocking, with a length more than twice its width. If California were superimposed on the East Coast, it would cover six states, from Florida to New York.[1] The enormous size of the state as well as recurrent battles over water supplies and financial resources have resulted in periodic proposals that the state be divided into two or even three separate states, with the presumption that the Northern, Central, and Southern regions could each stand alone as political entities.[2]

While California's size has contributed to its political dynamics, its location has been at least as important. As the leading state on what is called the Pacific Rim (those states bordering the Pacific Ocean and facing the Far East), 70 percent of California's international trade takes place with Asia, Australia, and New Zealand.[3] The state is also one of only 15 that border a foreign nation. In part as a result of proximity to Mexico,

Californians of Mexican descent have become the largest ethnic minority in the state, one that includes both first-generation Mexicans and "Chicanos" whose parents or ancestors originally came from Mexico.

Two other geographic influences command attention: rich natural resources and spectacularly beautiful terrain. Between the majestic Sierra Nevada range along the eastern border and the Coast Range on the west lies the Central Valley—one of the richest agricultural regions in the world. As a result, California leads the nation in farm output, although agriculture's political influence has diminished as urban residents and environmentalists have begun to win the water supply wars.[4] While over 40 percent of the state is forested, battles over environmental standards and redwood preservation have somewhat reduced the power of the lumber industry and caused lengthy litigation.[5] California has plentiful oil, yet even the once invincible petroleum industry has occasionally been prevented from building pipelines through urban areas by *grassroots* organizations concerned about safety. While agriculture, timber, and oil remain economically important as well as environmentally controversial, another natural resource is also the subject of continual political debate over how much to exploit it: California's landscape. Ranging across arid deserts, a thousand-mile shoreline, and remote mountain wilderness, the terrain itself has become a battlefield between conservationists and commercial recreation developers. About 45 percent of all land is government owned (including 6 national parks and 17 national forests) compared with less than 34 percent in the entire nation.

Demographic Influences: Who Are We?

In recent years, California's population patterns have fluctuated. In contrast to the 1980s, when the state's population boomed, the 1990s have seen a slowing of population growth.[6] When the recession hit in 1990, many laid-off Californians set a pattern of *outmigration* by moving away from the state, yet foreign immigration continued to expand. By the mid-1990s, demographers began to project a return to higher growth as news of the economic recovery spread. Long-term predictions suggest that the state will have nearly 50 million people by the year 2025, with 60 percent of them being Latino or Asian.[7] Figure 2.1 breaks down the workforce by ethnic group. Meanwhile, despite brief periods of slowed growth, California remains the most populous state, with over 12 percent of the nation's people.[8]

The migration patterns of the 1990s have created interesting demographics. Those leaving the state tend to be white while those arriving are from all over the world, contributing to the extraordinary racial and cultural diversity of the state. The special needs of foreign immigrants for education, health care, transportation, and other services created fierce debates during the recession when government revenues were

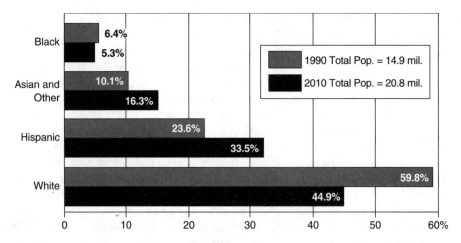

Figure 2.1   California Labor Force by Ethnic Group, 1990–2010: Percentage of Labor Force Population.

Source: Center for Continuing Study of the California Economy.

tight. To a certain extent, that debate continues as the economy improves, but with more focus on the relationship between federal and state responsibility for immigrants. This competition over scarce resources certainly contributed to the 1994 victory of Proposition 187, a largely unconstitutional attempt to deny public services to undocumented immigrants and their children, many of whom are U.S. citizens.

The racial and ethnic diversity of the state's population will probably continue to increase. Many of the foreign immigrants come from Mexico, Central America, and the Asian Pacific region, with substantial numbers arriving from Russia, the Middle East, and the Caribbean.[9] Unlike their predecessors of other eras, recent immigrants do not necessarily settle in urban areas but are increasingly integrating formerly "white" suburbs such as Santa Clarita and parts of Orange County.[10] During their *assimilation* into California's culture, immigrants can choose whether to become citizens and thus potential voters. Because of changes in federal law as well as the fear created by the passage of Proposition 187, *naturalization* rates are climbing as immigrants realize the value of becoming U.S. citizens.

Whether they are citizens or residents, immigrants have already altered the social and political landscape in many California communities. Out of choice or necessity, ethnic enclaves develop wherever immigrant groups put down roots, their presence reflected in the language of storefront signs, distinctive architecture, and types of food available. Daly City is called "Little Manila," and Fresno is home to 30,000 Hmong, members of a Laotian hill tribe. Stockton has 35,000 refugees from several areas of Indochina; Glendale has a substantial concentration of Armenians; Westminster, in Orange County, is known as "Little Seoul," and Monterey Park, the first city in the continental United States with an Asian majority,[11] is 56 percent Chinese. About 3 million Hispanics, mostly of Mexican descent, live in Los Angeles County, and the school-children there speak 80 different languages.[12]

While the debate over the role of immigrants continues, American-born ethnic minorities are often mistakenly lumped into the same categories as the newcomers. Because they share the same ethnic heritage as their immigrant relatives, American-born Latinos and Asians may be subject to similar prejudices and discrimination. Despite being U.S. citizens, many Latinos still face enormous obstacles in achieving adequate educations, while Asian Americans have often been stereotyped into "perfect student" roles that place burdens on those who do not fulfill that expectation. Recent studies show that newly arrived immigrant youth have the highest appreciation for education, while second-generation Americans of minority descent show signs of losing faith in their ability to achieve the California dream through hard work.[13] (See Table 2.1.) This may suggest that *acculturation* is a mixed blessing for immigrant children. Meanwhile, African Americans, the third-largest ethnic minority group, continue to see their numbers decline in proportion to the fast-growing Latino and Asian communities, with resulting concerns about how blacks can compete successfully for educational and political opportunities as other ethnic groups begin to dominate numerically.

Population diversity, of course, embraces far more than ethnicity. Collectively, Californians seem to embody virtually the whole range of

Table 2.1

Ranking of Average Income Among 30-Year-Old California Workers (Overall Average $32,861)

Category	Income
White males	$39,279
Asian male citizens	$35,361
Hispanic male citizens	$34,554
Black males	$30,842
White females	$28,938
Asian female citizens	$28,046
Black females	$26,588
Hispanic female citizens	$25,488
Asian male immigrants	$24,713
Hispanic male immigrants	$21,191
Hispanic female immigrants	$19,392
Asian female immigrants	$19,202

Source: McLeod, Ramon G. "White Women, Young Minorities Make Pay Gains," *San Francisco Chronicle,* 6 September 1993, p. 13.

religious beliefs, including nearly 20 percent who profess no religion at all. No "majority religion" exists in California, with 45 percent Protestant, 25 percent Roman Catholic, 5 percent Jewish, and 7 percent "other." About one-third of Californians claim to be "born-again Christians," which may partially account for the strength of the Christian Coalition, a political movement based on a belief that fundamentalist Christian theology should guide American politics.[14]

Another of California's diverse groupings is the gay community, often a target of the Christian Coalition. Although the state's antigay political movements are well organized, the gay rights movement also taps into a committed group of supporters. While there are no precise statistics on the numbers of gay and lesbian Californians, the growing political strength of the gay community indicates that there is enough of a base to support and elect gay candidates in certain areas. The state assembly now has two acknowledged lesbians, while numerous localities have gay and lesbian council members and school board members. Despite these visible electoral gains, *homophobia*, like racial prejudice, persists in varying degrees throughout the state, and acts of violence directed at gays have mobilized gay organizations to start their own safety patrols in some areas.

California's Political Culture: How We Think

Each state has a distinctive political style that is shaped not only by its geography and population characteristics but also by the values and attitudes shared by most of its people. These elements constitute what is sometimes called the political culture. In many ways, California is similar to the rest of the country and is conditioned by the same influences. Californians embrace the principles of patriotism, capitalism, and democracy as fervently as any Americans. But there are differences as well, stemming from both unique historical development and the steady emergence of distinctive problems demanding political attention. California's frontier heritage, for example, includes a legacy of materialistic individualism that may exceed that of most other states.

Perhaps this focus on the freedom to "cash in" and acquire the status symbols of California life (a pool, a Porsche, and a private school for the kids) has made California more of a *two-tier* state than some others. Inequality in household incomes is the highest in the nation, with the major cause being the decline in income of those at the bottom. More Californians are poor now than were poor in the late 1960s.[15] The increases in inequality were particularly intense during the *recession*, yet the impacts will not necessarily end just because the state is doing better as a whole. The good news lies in recent small-scale surveys which suggest that Californians' confidence in the state's economy grew substantially as the recession faded, with 80 percent of the 1,009 persons polled stating that they are satisfied with their standard of living.[16] At the same time, one in six children in the state lives without health insurance despite having working parents, who must often choose between purchasing medical care or paying the rent.[17]

Aggravating the gaps between rich and poor are the high cost of housing, the twenty-year decline in public K–12 education funding, and the continuing pressures of international competition. However, some of these factors have improved recently. After a long period of declining revenues, California's public schools have received new funds to reduce class size so that children can benefit from more individual attention from teachers. Housing costs, while never low, declined somewhat during the recession and have not returned to 1980s levels. Unemployment rates have dropped, and service industries as well as manufacturers have been satisfied with changes in state tax codes that permit them to remain in California yet continue to keep more of their profits.[18]

With this mix of economic good news and bad news, and the sense that the haves are doing much better than the have-nots, California's political climate is also mixed. After years of low voter turnout, the state may be seeing a slight increase in voting among certain groups. The *electorate*, which had been nearly 80 percent white, has seen a 37 percent increase in participation by Latino voters, many of whom are newly naturalized citizens eager to vote against politicians and ballot measures that promote *immigrant-bashing*.[19] At the local level, voters are increasingly supporting school *bond issues* along with bonds to provide funds for libraries and public safety. While large pockets of cynicism and mistrust of government exist, there may be some revival of a democratic spirit among those who realize the power of government to improve or to harm individual lives.

For some Californians, the recognition of government's power has caused them to form political associations to represent their views. Because of the ethnic, socioeconomic, and cultural diversity of the state, California is home to a wide variety of political views and organizations. The *conservative* side of California politics is torn between those who support maximum freedom for both business and individuals and those who like free enterprise but prefer government to regulate personal behavior such as sexuality and abortion. These uneasy partners form the basis of the California Republican party, and their areas of agreement often end with tax cuts and calls to *privatize* government services. Moderate Republicans, especially women, often feel stuck between their views on economic matters and their party's continuing domination by "cultural conservatives" who promote an antichoice, antigay, and antifeminist agenda.

On the other side of the political spectrum, the *liberal* movement in California has moved considerably to the center. Onetime genuine *left-wing* ideas, such as promoting social equality and government action to solve problems, are now modified to the point that they are nearly unrecognizable to those who promoted them during the mass movements of the 1960s. Yet some former student activists who turned UC Berkeley into a center of free speech and civil rights issues thirty years ago are now elected officials juggling the conflicting demands of California's diverse population. Perhaps the decline in political *polarization* will enable California to move more creatively into the new millennium. And perhaps the less intense political divisions will combine with the enlarged economic pie to encourage Californians and their elected representatives to consider how those who have achieved the California dream can assist those who are still working toward it.

Questions to Consider
Using Your Text and Your Own Experiences

1. What is the relationship between California's geography (size, location, topography, etc.) and its economic and political situation?

2. What are some of the pros and cons of the state's ethnic diversity?

3. Discuss the issue of social and economic inequality. What problems are caused by the vast gaps between rich and poor? Are there any advantages to having a two-tier society?

Notes

1. *Los Angeles Times*, 17 December 1987, sec. 1, p. 3.
2. Charles Price, "The Longshot Bid to Split California," *California Government and Politics Annual*, 1994–1995, p. 10.
3. MISER Series 1 data, California Trade and Commerce Agency, as cited in *California Journal*, July 1996, p. 26.
4. David Margolick, "As Drought Looms, Farmers in California Blame Politics," *New York Times*, national editions, 24 June 1994, p. A1.
5. John Skow, "Redwoods: The Last Stand," *Time*, 6 June 1994, p. 58.
6. Carl Ingram, "State's Population Increases only 1.4%," *Los Angeles Times*, 9 February 1994, p. A19.
7. David Westphal, "State's Population Growth Slowing," *Los Angeles Daily News*, 5 January 1997, p. 4.
8. Faye Fiore, "Population Surge of 18 Million Seen for State by 2025," *Los Angeles Times*, 25 August 1997, p. A1.
9. Julia Franco, "The Great Divide: Immigration in the 1990s," *Los Angeles Times*, 14 November 1993, p. A1.
10. Susan Goldsmith, "Immigrants Find American Dream in Suburbs," *Los Angeles Daily News*, 12 June 1994, p. 3.
11. Seth Mydans, "Asian Investors Create a Pocket of Prosperity," *New York Times*, 17 October 1994, p. A8.
12. *The Economist*, 13 October 1990, pp. 8–10.
13. Elaine Woo, "Immigrants, U.S. Peers Differ Starkly on Schools," *Los Angeles Times*, 22 February 1996, p. A1.
14. Mark Nollinger, "The New Crusaders: The Christian Right Storms California's Political Bastions," *California Journal*, January 1993, p. 6.

15. Deborah Reed, "Income Inequality in California Outpaces U.S.," *Public Affairs Report,* September 1996, p. 3.
16. Tom Petruno and Debora Vrana, "State Economy, Personal Finances Stir Optimism," *Los Angeles Times,* 21 February 1997, p. A1.
17. Julie Marquis, "'Shocking' Lack Cited in Child Health Insurance," *Los Angeles Times,* 19 March 1997, p. B1.
18. Tim W. Ferguson, "California's Comeback," *Forbes,* 20 November 1995, p. 141.
19. "California Latino Turnout Breaks All Records," *Southwest Voter Research Notes,* vol. 11, no. 2, Spring 1997, p. 1.

Chapter 3

California's Historical Development

California will try to get by as it has always gotten by . . . hoping that the regime of abundance will last forever, or at least for another generation.
—James D. Houston, California scholar

California's modern history begins with the native population of about 300,000 people in approximately 100 linguistic/cultural "tribelets" who lived on this land before the Europeans arrived.[1] Despite the unique culture of each of the dozens of Native California tribes, very little information exists regarding the diverse groups that inhabited California during this period. Perhaps that is because these first Californians were so nearly exterminated. According to a New York newspaper in 1860, "in (other) States, the Indians have suffered wrongs and cruelties. . . . But history has no parallel to the recent atrocities perpetrated in California. Even the record of Spanish butcheries in Mexico and Peru has nothing so diabolical."[2] The hunter-gatherers of California were virtually annihilated to make room for the *conquistadores*, whose desire for gold led them to murder and rape the indigenous people.[3]

The Spanish Era: 1542–1821

In 1542, only 50 years after Columbus first came to the "New" World, Spain claimed California as a result of a voyage by Juan Rodriguez Cabrillo. More than two centuries passed, however, before the Spanish established their first colony. It was named San Diego and founded by an expedition headed by Gaspar de Portola, a military commander, and Junipero Serra, a missionary dedicated to converting the Indians to Roman Catholicism. Between 1769 and 1823, the Spanish conquerors, using Indian slave labor, built a series of missions running the length of California from San Diego to San Francisco, each with its own military post. By the time the missions were completed, most of the native cultures had been eradicated or severely distorted by the demands of Catholicism, and the *mestizo* residents of New Spain (which actually included most of Central America and Mexico as well as the U.S. Southwest) were ready to overthrow the Spanish colonial rulers and declare independence.

Mexican Dominance: 1821–1848

In 1832, after a decade-long war against Spain, newly independent Mexico claimed California as part of its national territory. Civilian governments were established for the pueblos, or villages, but the distant government in Mexico City still viewed California as a remote and relatively unimportant colony. American settlers began to arrive in the 1840s, lured by the inviting climate and stories of economic opportunities. Many were imbued with the spirit of "*Manifest Destiny*," a belief that Americans had a mission to control the whole continent. When the United States failed in its attempt to buy California, it used a Texas boundary dispute as an excuse to launch the Mexican War in 1846. The war ended within a year with the United States winning enormous lands, including California, Arizona, New Mexico, and Texas as well as large parts of Utah, Colorado, and Nevada. California came under U.S. military rule, and in 1848 Mexico renounced its claims by signing the Treaty of Guadalupe Hidalgo, a document which promised the Mexican population of California that their language and property would be respected under the new government. The current state flag is the only permanent legacy of the brief "Bear Flag Revolt" (1846) launched by American settlers who wanted California to become an independent nation instead of a U.S. territory.

Americanization and Statehood: 1848–1850

The U.S. military occupation lasted three years. Congress, which normally places newly acquired lands under territorial government, was immobilized by a dispute over whether to permit slavery in its newest possession. Before the issue could be settled, gold was discovered in 1848, making California land the most highly prized in the entire world. In 1849, the year of the legendary Gold Rush, the settlers adopted the first California constitution, largely pieced together from constitutional fragments adopted earlier by Iowa and New York. The Compromise of 1850, enacted by Congress, temporarily settled the slavery issue by admitting California as a free state, making it the thirty-first in the Union and the first that did not border an existing state. (Figure 3.1 shows the county boundaries of California today.)

Today the legacy of the Spanish and Mexican periods can be found in California's architecture, place names, and food. But the character of state government is clearly based on Anglo-American traditions.

Figure 3.1   Map of California.

Source: Los Angeles County Almanac, 1991.

Consolidating Power: 1850–1902

During its first fifty years of statehood, California grew in both population and diversity. Newcomers from around the world came to seek their fortunes, and some were extraordinarily successful. Others, particularly during economic downturns, began to *scapegoat* less popular groups and call for their expulsion. Chinese immigrants, brought to this country to build the railroads cheaply, were major targets of overt racism and discrimination during the recession of the 1870s. Despite periods of decline, the overall economy boomed during this period, although the *Californios,* or those of Mexican descent, generally became impoverished and forgotten as white Americans took charge. The economy shifted from mining to agriculture, and the arrival of the transcontinental railroad increased the frenzied population growth as well as the lust for power among those who owned the rails.

In 1879 the first state constitution was replaced by the one now in effect. In a preview of political events that would recur over 100 years later, the second California constitution was loaded with anti-immigrant provisions (aimed at Asian immigrants) later declared invalid as violations of the U.S. Constitution.

The Progressive Legacy: 1902–1919

The *Progressive movement* in California, like its national counterpart, arose at the beginning of the twentieth century. Its goal was to reduce the power of corrupt political parties and rich corporations that spent large sums to control politicians. In California, the primary target was the Southern Pacific Railroad, a corporation that owned one-fifth of all nonpublic land in the state. Its major stockholders—Charles Crocker, Leland Stanford, Collis P. Huntington, and Mark Hopkins—were the "Big Four" of state politics. According to their critics, they had bought "the best state legislature that money could buy."

Despite the power of the Big Four, the Progressives had remarkable success. Child labor laws and conservation policies were adopted. Political parties were weakened when rigid legal controls were imposed on their internal organization and candidates for city, county, school board, and judicial office were prohibited from revealing their party affiliations on the ballot. Today, all of these offices remain *nonpartisan.*

Possibly the most important legacies left by the Progressives were the *initiative* powers, which permit voters to pass laws or amend the state constitution through the ballot box, and the *recall,* which enables voters to remove an elected official from office through a special election.

Constitutional Principles and Practices

Like the national government, the California political system is characterized by freedom, democracy, and a separation of powers. Certain differences, however, deserve attention. Although the separation of powers involves the traditional three branches—legislative, executive, and judicial—each is marked by distinctive state characteristics. The California legislature, for example, shares lawmaking authority with the people through the initiative process; the governor's power is diminished by the popular election of seven other executive officials; and lower-court judges are chosen by the voters for six-year terms (although most of them begin their judicial careers as gubernatorial appointees).

The separation of powers, designed to prevent too much power from falling into the hands of too few people, has been marvelously successful in preventing tyranny. But it also has prevented prompt, effective action in dealing with major issues. This is particularly true when the governor belongs to one party and a majority in the legislature belongs to the other party—a situation that California voters seem to create frequently. Unsolved problems that voters perceive to be the result of incompetence or indifference on the part of public officials may be instead the consequence of a deadlock reflecting serious and sincere disagreements between Republicans and Democrats.

Many of the freedoms guaranteed in the state constitution are identical to those protected by the U.S. Constitution. However the state constitution includes additional rights for its residents. For example, Article I, Section 1 of the California Constitution proclaims, "All people are by nature free and independent and have inalienable rights. Among these are enjoying and defending life and liberty, acquiring, possessing, and protecting property, and pursuing and obtaining safety, happiness, and privacy." Similar references to property acquisition, safety, happiness, and privacy are nowhere to be found in the U.S. Constitution.

California's constitution is much easier to amend than the federal Constitution, and it has been amended (and thus lengthened) over 500 times since 1879. The process involves two steps. First, amendments may be proposed either by a two-thirds vote in both houses of the legislature or by an initiative petition signed by 8 percent of the number of voters who voted in the last election for governor. Second, the proposed amendment must appear as a proposition on the ballot and must be approved by a simple majority of voters. Due to the options created by the Progressives, voters can amend the state constitution without any legislative action.

Because the authors of initiative measures, as well as the voters, rarely distinguish between propositions that create laws and those that amend the constitution, the document has been burdened with many policies that should be *statutes* rather than parts of the permanent state charter. Because over the years the state constitution has become excessively long and detailed, and because so many aspects of state government seem to be inefficient or unresponsive to the public, a Constitution Revision Commission recently spent several years developing proposals for a major overhaul of the document. However, since the report was presented in 1996, there has been little effort to implement it, probably due to the same political fragmentation and divisions that the document itself encourages.

Questions to Consider

Using Your Text and Your Own Experiences

1. Who were the first Californians? Why were they so thoroughly destroyed by those who came next?

2. What is the most important contribution of the Progressive movement in California?

3. What are some ways in which California's history affects life today? Consider culture, politics, ethnic diversity, immigration, and so on.

Notes

1. Sucheng Chan and Spencer Olin, *Major Problems in California History*. Boston: Houghton Mifflin, 1997, p. 30.
2. Cited by Alexander Cockburn, "Beat the Devil," *The Nation*, 24 June 1991, p. 839.
3. Antonia I. Castaneda, "Spanish Violence Against Amerindian Women," from Adela de la Torre and Beatriz Pesquera, eds., *Building with Our Hands: New Directions in Chicana Studies*. Berkeley: University of California Press, 1993.

Chapter

4

Freedom and Equality: California's Delicate Balance

California is not so much poor as it is unequal.
—Robert Enoch Buck, sociologist

People in California, as everywhere else in a capitalist democracy, must continually reassess choices regarding personal freedom and social equality. *Civil liberties*, such as the freedoms of speech, press, and association (which restrict government powers), may conflict with *civil rights*, which often require government protections. For example, freedom of association can conflict with antidiscriminatory civil rights laws. Even though the state's Unruh Civil Rights Act was passed in 1959, some clubs and individuals are still claiming First Amendment freedom as reason to exclude women, unmarried couples, atheists, and homosexuals. In *Warfield v. Peninsula Golf and Country Club*, a Northern California woman received a favorable state Supreme Court decision that determined that she could become a member of this all-male club, and in *Smith v. Fair Housing*, an unmarried couple received the court's support in their lawsuit against a landlord who refused to rent to them because they were "living in sin." California court rulings also include the controversial decision to permit the state's Boy Scouts to exclude atheists.[1]

Freedom and Social Responsibility: Juggling Between Extremes

In numerous areas where individual freedom may conflict with public safety, California's policies have often shifted gradually from endorsing maximum personal freedom to placing some limits on that freedom in order to maximize the well-being of the larger society. After many years of debate, the state legislature passed a law to create statewide antismoking standards while allowing cities to enact even stricter standards. The smoking lobby, spearheaded by the Tobacco Institute, spent over $18 million fighting the legislation and then attempting a deceptive ballot initiative to overturn it, but public health concerns prevailed over the "freedom to smoke" arguments.[2] Similar public health measures include the helmet laws for motorcyclists and bicyclists, the life vest law for children on boats, and the controversial law banning assault rifles. In a recent case, the state Supreme Court ruled that public safety was more important than individual privacy when it upheld the right of the city of Glendale to require certain job applicants to submit to drug and alcohol tests.[3]

In the arena of environmental quality, affecting even more Californians, the South Coast Air Quality Management District (SCAQMD) has had to walk a fine line between protecting public health and protecting business. During its earlier years, the SCAQMD Board passed strict regulations to clean up the air, but well-organized business interests argued that the region's economy was being strangled by regulation. Recently, the agency has revised its clean air goals and expedited business permits even as environmentalists claim that public health is being endangered by the agency's new "pro-business" approach. Meanwhile, the federal government continues to monitor California's gradual compliance with federal clean air regulations, and both businesses and environmentalists are watching closely as the first electric (nonpolluting) vehicles go into operation in California.

In yet another arena, California courts have ruled that personal freedom includes the right *not* to hear a prayer at a public school graduation ceremony. In deference to the vast diversity of religious beliefs among Californians, the state Supreme Court determined that such prayers and invocations are an establishment of religion in violation of the separation of church and state.

Equality: A Long Way to Go

Along with their controversial struggles over personal freedom and societal responsibility, Californians have also been forced to confront a long history of racial bigotry. Prejudiced attitudes and discriminatory behaviors are older than the state itself. Only 10 percent of the Native Californians survived the Spanish era, and the first governor after statehood called for the extermination of those who remained. When the United States defeated Mexico in 1848, California Mexicans were gradually marginalized, losing much of the political and economic power they once wielded. Soon after, in the period of economic stagnation of the 1870s, the Chinese immigrants who helped build the transcontinental railroads during the 1860s became the targets of serious forms of racism, including lynchings and the "Chinese exclusion" provision of the 1879 state constitution (which attempted to prohibit Chinese from holding many kinds of jobs).

In today's multicultural California, the issues of equity are more complex than ever. With the passage of Proposition 209, the initiative to end affirmative action programs in all public agencies, the public polarized between those who believe that racial and ethnic discrimination still exists and must be remedied by conscious efforts and those who believe enough has been done for minorities already. Opponents of the proposition took their concerns to court, but the U.S. Supreme Court ruled that Proposition 209 was constitutional, thus ending a thirty-year effort to increase the proportion of underrepresented groups in public institutions.

Meanwhile, racial tensions exist not only between whites and various minorities, but among minority groups themselves. In urban school districts, high schools have been closed temporarily due to clashes between Latinos and African Americans, while interethnic gang rivalry remains a deadly problem in some California cities. During the 1992 uprising in Los Angeles, the participants represented all ethnic groups, but the media focused on tensions between black and Korean residents. Even inside the prison system, inmates of different ethnic groups are segregated as a technique to avoid violence.

The conflicts among many of California's ethnic groups no doubt reflect the continuing difficulties that all people of color have in competing for scarce opportunities. (See Figure 4.1.) Although the law prohibits discrimination in employment, subtle limitations exist for nonwhite groups. In the rapidly expanding and highly competitive entertainment industry, opportunities for people of color continue to be rare. Despite the handful of well-known blacks and Latinos in the field, membership statistics for both the Writers Guild of America and the Screen Actors Guild indicate the work yet to be done on fully integrating these poten-

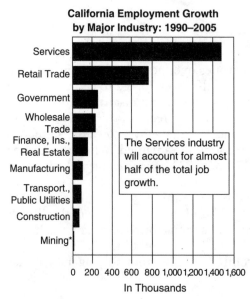

California Employment Growth by Major Industry: 1990–2005

The Services industry will account for almost half of the total job growth.

0   200 400 600 800 1,000 1,200 1,400 1,600
In Thousands

Figure 4.1 Targeting Training to Industry and Occupational Trends.

˙Mining employment is projected to decline by 2,000.

Source: Employment Development Department, Labor Market Division.

tially lucrative fields. A full 98 percent of the Writers Guild members are white,[4] while the Screen Actors Guild membership is 85 percent white.[5] Both unions have affirmative action programs and training opportunities for minorities, but as in most fields, the subtleties of prejudice will take many years to erase.

Similar problems exist in the housing market. Despite court decisions and a long-standing state law known as the Rumford Fair Housing Act, hundreds of landlords apparently continue to discriminate on the basis of race or ethnicity. In 1990, Beaumont Property Company, with control of 10,000 apartments throughout Southern California, was held liable for a $317,000 settlement to the Fair Housing Congress, which represented minorities who had received "significantly different treatment" when seeking apartments.[6] The terms of the settlement also required the company to retrain its employees so that they understood and obeyed all civil rights laws.

Patterns of housing discrimination lead to segregation in schools. As recently as fifty years ago, it was completely legal to segregate African Americans and Mexican Americans into separate schools. Despite court rulings that eliminated legal segregation, public schools in California remain highly segregated for these two groups, and the numerous private schools that have developed in response to the problems of public education are even more segregated. Test scores, graduation rates, college admission data, and other indicators of educational success are almost always lower at public schools attended by minorities (typically from low-income families), and the continuing debate about bilingual education is evidence that no one has proved how best to educate the millions of students whose English is limited. Table 4.1 shows that almost one-fourth of the state's adults have not graduated from high school. At the

Table 4.1

Educational Attainment of Persons 18 Years of Age and Older, California, 1990 Census

Educational Attainment Level	Number	Percentage
Total persons	22,020,542	100.0
Less than 9th grade	2,352,017	10.7
9th to 12th grade, no diploma	3,114,969	14.1
High school graduate (includes equivalency)	5,080,909	23.1
Some college, no degree	5,246,699	23.8
Associate degree	1,649,596	7.5
Bachelor's degree	3,052,702	13.9
Graduate or professional degree	1,523,650	6.9

Source: 1990 Census of Population and Housing, Summary Tape File 3A.

university level, the decision by the Regents of the University of California to end affirmative action (before Proposition 209 passed) has already caused sharp reductions in the numbers of blacks and Latinos entering the UC system, particularly the prestigious law and medical schools.[7]

Diversity in Representation: Identity Politics in Action

With equality a long way off in so many areas, it is no surprise that there has not been much increase in minority political power. Even the term "minority" is a misnomer and should no longer be used the way it once was. By the year 2025, whites will make up about one-third of the population and will thus be a "minority" group, while Latinos and Asians together will compose 60 percent (43 and 17 percent, respectively).[8] However, this *demographic shift* will not necessarily create an equally rapid shift in political power. Gains for underrepresented groups depend on much more than their mere numbers. Factors that influence access to political power include their rates of voter registration and turnout, their financial ability to support candidates, and their interest in the political process. One structural change that appears to be helping more diverse candidates to win election is the voter-approved term limits law, which creates mandatory turnover in the state legislature and executive branch.

Although underrepresented groups may gradually benefit from term limits, their overall political effectiveness has been diminished by several factors. One is the lack of financial clout of many ethnic communities. Because they are often excluded from well-paying jobs, they do not have the resources to support or recruit their own candidates. In addition, although blacks and native-born Latinos and Asians are citizens and eligible to vote, many of the new immigrants are not, thus losing out on the most fundamental political opportunity, the *franchise*. Despite the obstacles, changes have already begun in the distribution of political power among ethnic groups. The 1996 elections marked an important turning point for Latinos as they voted in historically large numbers and helped elect a record-breaking number of legislators from their communities. Statewide, including every level of government, there are over 800 Latinos in elected office.[9] Latino assembly members, along with colleagues of other backgrounds, made history when they elected Cruz Bustamante as their speaker, the first Latino in California history to win this important position.

As Latinos increase numerically, they have begun to live in many neighborhoods traditionally represented by African American politicians. Over time it appears that African Americans will decline numerically in proportion to the much faster-growing Latino and Asian groups, and African American leaders are concerned about maintaining adequate representation. Some black politicians have made it a point to learn Spanish as a way to bridge the gap with their Latino constituents.

Asian Americans, in part because they do not tend to live in concentrated areas, are not electing members of their group in large numbers, yet they are beginning to see gains at the local level. Like Latinos, whose numbers include people of 18 different nationalities, Asian Americans represent over 30 distinct national origins. Because the diversity is so enormous, there will never be precise and proportional representation for every ethnic group. Therefore, elected officials, regardless of their own backgrounds, must learn to represent everyone in their districts and not appeal to narrow ethnic concerns.

In addition to the largest ethnic and racial groups, small but active minority communities are working toward having a greater share of political power. Armenian Californians have seen a governor from their heritage elected, while California's growing Islamic population has learned that not a single Muslim holds public office in California.[10] Native Americans in California, who compose over 120 tribal groups, have focused their political attention on issues relating to economic development on tribal land (with a heavy emphasis on building gambling casinos) and protection of their culture. With the state's social diversity likely to continue, politics in the twenty-first century will be a rainbow of cultures, with leaders who must retain their unique identities while also working to represent all Californians.

Sexual Politics: Slow Change for the Underrepresented

Women have made slow progress since the women's liberation movement of the 1960s raised concerns about women's equality and access to power. While women are 51 percent of the population, they are nowhere near having half of legislative seats, executive positions, judgeships, or local posts. Nonetheless, there are more women in office than at any other time in California history, with 7 women representatives (out of 40) in the Senate and 20 (out of 80) in the Assembly. The state Supreme Court now has 3 women justices (out of 7). Meanwhile, at the nonelected level, thousands of women who are state employees in agencies ranging from the Department of Motor Vehicles to the Employment Development Department earn only about three-fourths as much as men doing the same jobs.[11]

In a symbolic moment, the state's congressional delegation broke national records when Californians elected 2 women senators, Barbara Boxer and Dianne Feinstein. They are joined in Washington, D.C., by 10 women (out of California's 52) in the House of Representatives. Since there are currently no term limits for members of Congress, these women may remain in office for many years.

One often invisible and perhaps underrepresented minority group is the gay and lesbian community. At one time, openly gay politicians were rare outside San Francisco or West Hollywood, both magnets for the homosexual population. Now the state assembly has two "open" lesbian members, and numerous local governments have gay and lesbian elected officials. As more gays come *"out of the closet"* and become politically active, their clout will no doubt increase. However, the gay community remains divided politically, with many conservative gays wanting to change the "gay power" approach to politics and lifestyles.

California's record of electing politicians with diverse backgrounds is certainly better than that of many other states. But perhaps it is inevitable that California take the lead, since the demographic pattern of increasing diversity is unlikely to change, and trends suggest that the nation will gradually come to look more like California in the twenty-first century.

Questions to Consider
Using Your Text and Your Own Experiences

1. Discuss some of the areas in which individual freedom (or free enterprise) may conflict with social needs. What is your position on these issues?

2. In what arenas are ethnic "minorities" underrepresented? Why do these patterns persist even though California has no "majority" group?

3. What can be done to balance the needs of diverse ethnic groups with the needs of California as a whole?

Notes

1. Taylor Flynn (attorney, Southern California American Civil Liberties Union), Interview by author, 30 June 1997.
2. Dan Morain and Virginia Ellis, "Tobacco Industry Power May Go Up in Smoke, Foes Say," *Los Angeles Times*, 10 November 1994, p. A3.
3. Maura Dolan, "Jurists Uphold Drug Testing by Employees," *Los Angeles Times*, 7 January 1997, p. A3.
4. Writers Guild of America, Human Resources Department, Membership Records, 1989.
5. Rodney Mitchell (Executive Director, Affirmative Action Department, Screen Actors Guild), Interview by author, 1994.
6. Judy Pasternak, "Firm Must Pay $317,000, Settle Bias Lawsuit," *Los Angeles Times*, 19 December 1990, p. A18.
7. Kenneth R. Weiss, "Plans Seek More UC Pupils from Poorer Schools," *Los Angeles Times*, 12 May 1997, p. A1.
8. David Westphal, "State's Population Growth Slowing," *Los Angeles Daily News*, 5 January 1997, p. 4.
9. Mark Z. Barabak, "A New Breed of Latino Lawmaker," *Los Angeles Times*, 16 July 1997, p. A1.
10. Salam al-Marayati, (Director, Muslim Public Affairs Council of Los Angeles), Interview by author, Glendale, 21 May 1997.
11. "State's Female Workers Paid Less Than Men, Study Finds," *Los Angeles Times*, 25 April 1996, p. A21.

Chapter

5

Media Influences and Pressure Groups

The power of the [media] determines what people will talk about and think about.

—Theodore White

In a democratic system, the attitudes of the public should be a primary basis for political decision making. These political attitudes are demonstrated in election results and develop from opinions formed by the influence of families, friends, religious institutions, schools, life experiences, the mass media, and pressure groups. In recent years, as Americans read less, television and radio talk shows and "chat rooms" on the Internet no doubt help shape public opinion in the way that newspapers once did. In a large and diverse state such as California, organized interest groups and the enormous number of media outlets are vital components of the political process.

The Mass Media: A Massive Influence

Although state government profoundly affects peoples' daily lives, most media tend to neglect state and local news in favor of more dramatic national and international events. Despite the massive coverage of the O. J. Simpson trial in a Los Angeles superior court, California's television and radio stations usually provide little reporting from Sacramento or the various county or city halls around the state. The only ongoing TV coverage of state politics is the legislature's own television program, which shows legislative proceedings on many cable stations throughout California. The larger newspapers cover state politics, while many of the local issues are reported primarily in smaller papers. For the fortunate few with computer skills and access, information on legislative action is available over the Internet; California posts timely information and permits the public to e-mail elected officials through the Web.[1] (See Appendix C for Web sites.)

Because of California's size, creating an image that is memorable and appealing to voters requires those running for statewide office to use the mass media extensively. Due to general social trends that have minimized newspaper reading and encouraged the public's heavy reliance on television and radio, candidates spend most of their funds for ads in the broadcast media even as they attempt to get editorial endorsements from newspapers. With the growth of the Internet, some candidates are trying to spread their message through Web sites and e-mail, a relatively inexpensive way to reach people.

Image making is serious business in California—more than $40 million was spent in the 1994 U.S. Senate election, primarily for television ads,[2] and it is estimated that 90 percent of California voters make their voting choices based on television advertising.[3] With the growth of cable television and the many channels available to viewers, politicians and their consultants are becomingly increasingly sophisticated in "niche programming": creating ads targeted for very specific audiences and shown only on certain channels. Critics charge that political information conveyed by the media emphasizes personality factors, attacks, and scandals rather than significant policy differences.

Economic Interest Groups: Pressure Where It Counts

Organized *pressure groups* are also important in shaping public opinion. These have been unusually influential in California politics and often aid individual candidates by providing them with publicity, financial contributions, and campaign workers. The most powerful groups are usually those with the most financial resources, including the majority of business interests and some of the larger unions, among them public school teachers and state prison guards. A group that supports a successful candidate gains better access to that politician than most average individuals ever have.

Special interest groups generally avoid direct affiliation with any political party, preferring instead to work with whichever politician is in office. Business groups usually prefer to help elect Republicans, while labor groups prefer Democrats. The influence of various interest groups is indicated, in part, by their wealth and the number of people who belong to or are employed by their organizations. (See Table 5.1.) Nearly all of California's most profitable corporations, including oil companies, insurance giants, utilities, banks, and telecommunications businesses, are linked together in pressure groups such as the California Manufacturers Association, the Western States Petroleum Association, and the Association of California Insurance Companies.[4] Other major *private sector* players in the lobby game are the California Association of Realtors, the California Medical Association, the Trial Lawyers Association, and the Agricultural Producers. The California Teachers Association, the California Correctional Peace Officers Association, the California State

Lobbying Expenses, January 1995–December 1996, by Industry

Industry	Total	Top Spender in Category	Amount
Agriculture	$6,153,211	California Farm Bureau	$1,156,404
Education	$16,117,939	California Teachers Association	$1,985,108
Entertainment/ recreation	$6,727,759	Circus Circus	$1,067,859
Banking/ insurance	$28,965,837	State Farm Insurance	$1,859,395
Government	$36,947,670	San Diego County	$1,479,159
Health	$30,831,649	California Care Health Plans	$849,836
Labor unions	$8,736,787	California School Employees Association	$1,599,545
Legal	$5,714,396	California Applicants' Attorneys	$838,381
Lodging/ restaurants	$938,092	California Restaurants Association	$344,224
Manufacturing/ industrial	$28,459,113	California Manufacturers Association	$1,707,477
Merchandise/ retail	$3,173,226	Robinson's-May	$468,014
Miscellaneous	$28,569,220	California Chamber of Commerce	$2,100,380
Oil and gas	$15,220,828	Western States Petroleum Association	$3,883,845
Political organizations	$728,496	California Federation of Republican Women	$144,928
Professional/trade	$18,722,322	California Motor Car Dealers Association	$1,063,187
Public employees	$4,038,691	Peace Officers Research Association	$639,910
Real estate	$6,087,409	Irvine Company	$745,572
Transportation	$5,170,784	Atchison, Topeka, & Santa Fe Railroad	$263,083
Utilities*	$15,636,128	California Cogeneration Council	$926,290
Total: All Lobbies	**$266,939,559**		

*Total expenditures by utilities include, in many cases, payments made in connection with administrative testimony before the California Public Utilities Commission.

Source: California Secretary of State, available from http://www.ss.ca.gov/prd/lexp/table1.htm

Employees Association, the California Labor Federation, and many other groups represent labor interests, not necessarily in a unified manner.

The ability of special interest groups to give massive amounts of campaign donations has been challenged repeatedly by ballot initiatives such as Proposition 208 (1996). This proposition, since declared unconstitutional, imposed strict limits on donations to candidates. Within a year, the courts ruled it illegal (because campaign money is a form of "free speech" that cannot be restricted), and major fundraising immediately began again.

Other Interest Groups: Less Money, But Still a Voice

In addition to the business, professional, and labor groups that spend money to elect candidates through their *political action committees* (PACs) and later make contact with elected officials to share their views, less affluent interest groups also participate in California's political process. Such groups, discussed in Chapter 6, include those representing various ethnic communities; environmental organizations, such as the Planning and Conservation League; Children Now, which concerns itself with the needs of youth; and single-issue groups such as the California Abortion Rights Action League, Handgun Control, the Fund for Animals, and Surfriders (whose primary interest is in protecting beaches).

Various government agencies also lobby for their concerns. Numerous cities, counties, and special districts, such as water agencies and school districts, have paid lobbyists in Sacramento. These government entities are often seeking funding or other legislative support from the state capitol.

Lobbyists in Action: A High-Skill, High-Pay Career

The term *lobbying* began when those who wanted to influence elected officials would congregate in the lobbies of public buildings and wait to speak with a politician about their concerns. California's lobbyists, like those around the nation, gradually developed a pattern of wining and dining the politicians as well as giving them gifts and campaign contributions. Periodic scandals in which lobbyists and legislators are convicted of crimes involving trading money for votes create public demands for reform of the lobbying industry. The 1974 Political Reform Act requires each lobbyist to file monthly reports showing income, expenditures, and steps taken to influence government action. This initiative also created the Fair Political Practices Commission (FPPC), which oversees campaigns and lobbying and monitors any wrongdoing by candidates or PACs. Unfortunately, records of these expenditures are not easily available to voters. Over the years, voters have continued to support initiatives that have presented a variety of solutions to the problem of money-driven politics, but most of their impact has been blunted by court decisions ruling all or part of the initiatives invalid. (See Figure 5.1.)

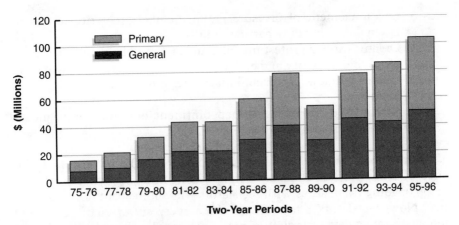

Figure 5.1 History of Campaign Costs: 1975–1996 Primary and General Election Candidates for the State Legislature.

Source: California Department of Finance.

One result of the money–politics connection is that increasing numbers of wealthy individuals, often with no political experience, are deciding that they should run for office because they can afford to purchase a well-financed campaign. The gubernatorial campaign of Al Checchi illustrates this situation well. Such individuals can then claim to be independent of the special interest groups whose dollars must fund more traditional, nonwealthy candidates. However, in cases where these affluent individuals actually win office, traditional lobbyists waste no time in gaining access, and they are often joined in their influence-peddling by the longtime business associates of the untrained politician.

In order to achieve their organizations' goals, lobbyists perform an assortment of tasks. Many lobbyists are former lawmakers or legislative aides whose personal contacts enable them to work successfully in the halls of power. They earn substantial salaries for handling the tasks listed below.

1. Campaign efforts to elect sympathetic candidates, especially incumbents.
2. Testimony for or against bills being considered by legislative committees.
3. Informal contacts with lawmakers for purposes of providing them with information, statistical data, and expert opinions on pending legislation.
4. Newspaper and other advertising designed to influence public officials indirectly by molding public opinion.
5. Sponsorship of initiative petitions to put propositions on the ballot for the approval of the voters.

6. Encouragement of pressure group members to write letters to lawmakers regarding particular bills.
7. Organization of protest marches and other public demonstrations.
8. Favorable publicity and endorsements for cooperative lawmakers inserted in newspapers and magazines circulated to organization members.
9. Attempts to influence the appointment of sympathetic judges and administrative officials.

With the passage of term limits (Proposition 140) in 1990, the influence of lobbyists has changed. Before term limits, lobbyists could develop ongoing friendships with legislators who often spent decades in office. Now, legislators rotate out of office every six or eight years, and lobbyists must develop relationships with newly elected officials and their new staff members on a frequent basis. However, those newly elected officials may be more susceptible to lobbyists because lobbyists have much more experience in Sacramento than most new legislators.

Because lobbying still determines the outcome of almost all legislation, Californians who realize how political decisions can affect their daily lives usually become interested in tracking the impact of lobbying on their elected officials. This involves checking campaign donation records and legislators' voting records in order to find out how a particular group has influenced a specific legislator. Because lobbying efforts fluctuate depending on which issues are "hot," voters must also watch for overall patterns in campaign contributions and subsequent votes by legislators. A major source of information is the secretary of state's quarterly report on lobbyists' expenses. Anyone interested in getting even more recent information can join interest groups that reflect the individual's values and political concerns. Many lobbies are open groups that welcome new members; these include organizations involved with environmental issues, ethnic concerns, health care, and many more. (See Appendix A.) Members receive updates from lobbyists indicating what legislation is being considered and how the member can phone or write in a timely, informed manner. While any individual Californian can always write a letter, the most effective political action comes through organized groups.

Questions to Consider
Using Your Text and Your Own Experiences

1. In how many ways do mass media influence political attitudes? Give examples of those influences.

2. What makes a special interest group powerful? Are there problems with how much power some of these groups have?

3. What can you do to have a voice in California's political process?

Notes

1. Max Vanzi, "Now Online, Legislature Goes Further," *Los Angeles Times*, 27 July 1997, p. A3.
2. Dave Lesher and Glenn F. Bunting, "Feinstein Is Apparent Winner in Senate Race," *Los Angeles Times*, 10 November 1994, p. A1.
3. B. Drummond Ayres, Jr., "Ad Nauseam: Campaigns Take Over California TV," *New York Times*, 14 October 1994, p. 1.
4. Douglas Frantz, "Is Bigger Better?" *Los Angeles Times*, 24 April 1988, p. B2.

Chapter 6

Political Parties and Other Voluntary Associations

*The success of the Republican and Democratic parties is gauged by how they do
at election time; electing their candidates is their primary focus.*
                                        —Ken deBow and John Syer, political scientists

The two major parties seem to be of even less importance to the average
Californian than to most Americans. Often they neither command loyalty nor determine ballot choices for major offices. Many citizen activists remain almost entirely separate from party organizations yet are
immersed in the grassroots political process through an enormous variety of voluntary associations, some of which, like many parent-teacher
associations (PTAs) and homeowner groups, have become highly politi-
cized. Activities that used to require volunteers with time and energy
and little political awareness now require participants who understand
the intimate links between one's neighborhood problems or local school
issues and the larger California political process. Parents of children in
dilapidated schools, homeowners concerned about graffiti, and beach
lovers whose shores are polluted are among many Californians whose
political involvement begins when they collect signatures for ballot initiatives or lobby public officials in an effort to resolve their particular
problems.

Meanwhile, despite the small numbers of Californians who participate directly in their political parties or feel any special enthusiasm for
either party, *party affiliations* are reflected in the voting patterns of legislators and the track records of governors. On many issues of major public
concern, such as abortion, criminal justice, and funding for education,
the majority party in the legislature can heavily influence the final outcome—and the votes of individual legislators may depend more on party
allegiance than on any other factor.

Do Parties Matter? The Voters' Perspective

California's constitution has served to minimize the powers of the two major parties. In some states, many government jobs are given as *patronage* by elected officials to reward those in their party who helped them win office. However, California uses a *civil service system* in which 98 percent of all state government jobs are earned on the basis of competitive examinations. Therefore, party loyalty is not necessarily the path to a good government job. Another way the major parties are weakened by the state constitution is that all local offices (including city, county, and school boards) and all judicial elections are *nonpartisan,* with candidates listed by name and occupation and no mention of party affiliation. The ballot format itself, known as the *office-block* ballot, groups candidates under the heading of the office being contested rather than in columns divided according to party, and thus encourages voters to concentrate on individual candidates rather than voting a straight party ticket. The nonpartisan nature of most of California politics is best illustrated by the fact that only 179 of the 19,279 elective offices throughout the state are *partisan.*[1]

Although the parties are not as well organized or as meaningful to voters as they are in some other states, Californians display some partisan loyalty. Voters who register in a party often vote for their party's candidates without much thought, and the enormous campaign funds spent on media are often aimed at the 20 percent of voters who aren't registered with either major party. These votes are "up for grabs" or *swing votes.,* Table 6.1 shows that many voters are not affiliated with the major parties.

Differences between Democrats and Republicans show up very clearly on matters such as taxation, aid to low-income Californians, and other major fiscal battlegrounds in the legislative arena. Almost all Republicans continue to favor tax cuts for business and the wealthy while Democrats are somewhat more willing to maintain tax rates to support

Table 6.1

Voter Registration Patterns, 1950–1997, Showing Decreased Affiliation with Major Parties

	Democrat	Republican	Other Party	Decline to State
1950	58%	35%	1%	4%
1960	57%	38%	1%	3%
1970	55%	39%	2%	4%
1980	53%	34%	9%	3%
1990	49%	39%	9%	2%
1997	46%	35%	12%	5%

Source: Assembly Republican Caucus, California Secretary of State.

public education and other programs. Even as the two parties have their differences, the differences within them are perhaps equally important. Moderate Republicans are under severe pressure from the "Christian right" to adopt its social policies, while mainstream Democrats are reminded by their more liberal colleagues about issues of campaign reform and environmental protection.

With all the internal and interparty dissension, it is perhaps no wonder that many citizens register their disaffection by refusing to vote at all or by registering to vote without affiliating with either major party.

Minor Parties: Alternative Political Voices

Although the state constitution makes it exceedingly difficult for minor parties to get on the ballot, California voters manage to show their frustration with the two major parties in diverse ways. In 1995, about 47 percent of voters were registered as Democrats and 37 percent as Republicans, with the remaining 16 percent belonging to one of the six minor parties or registered "*Decline to state,*" indicating no party affiliation.[2] The six minor parties are the Libertarian (advocates of *minimalist* government), American Independent (extremely conservative), Peace and Freedom (social justice concerns), Natural Law (belief in meditation as a political solution), Reform (Ross Perot's party), and Green (environmental focus). These parties remain official parties with *ballot status* as long as they receive 2 percent of the vote for any statewide office.

Then there is the small minority of Californians who belong to the category "Other" and have identified themselves as members of parties known as "Halloween," "Let's Have A," "Utopian Immoralist," "Smash the State," "Marijuana," and numerous other inventive titles.[3] Despite the seeming frivolity of these fanciful (or imaginary) parties, the official minor parties occasionally pull enough votes away from a major-party candidate to cause an electoral surprise or *upset,* such as the 1996 victory of Democrat Scott Wildman over Republican John Geranios in the traditionally Republican 43rd Assembly district. Wildman won by only 192 votes, while the Libertarian candidate, Willard Michlin, took over 3,000 votes, most of them no doubt from Republican Geranios.[4]

Party Organization: Who Makes the Rules?

California's parties are regulated both by state law and by their own internal guidelines. The general structure of the two major parties is identical, with each one having a state central committee and 58 *county committees.* The most powerful nonelected official in each party is the state party chair; however, this individual is rarely well known by the general public.

Beyond these two committees, much of party organization is left to each party. Democrats have organized themselves into Assembly district committees, while Republicans rely primarily on county committees for their local activities. These activities include recruiting candidates, raising money, registering voters, and supporting party nominees in general elections. Before the passage of Proposition 198 (1996), which authorized *open* or *blanket primaries* (in which all candidates are listed on one ballot regardless of party affiliation), citizens voted in *closed primaries* in which only members of a party could obtain that party's list of choices. This system disenfranchised the nearly 20 percent of California voters who are not registered in either major party and also brought out the most extreme factions of the major parties (less fanatical voters often did not bother to vote in primary elections). The *open primary* created by Proposition 198 is so new that political scientists and politicians are not yet sure how it will affect voter decisions, but thus far, the courts have upheld the initiative. (See Figure 6.1.)

Because California parties are generally viewed as weak, the two major parties attempt to create stronger internal structures by promoting "clubs" or caucuses. The California Republican Assembly is the oldest of these groups, while the California Democratic Council is the Democratic party's largest club. Other small groupings include the Log Cabin Club (Republican gay rights group) and the Democrats for Neighborhood

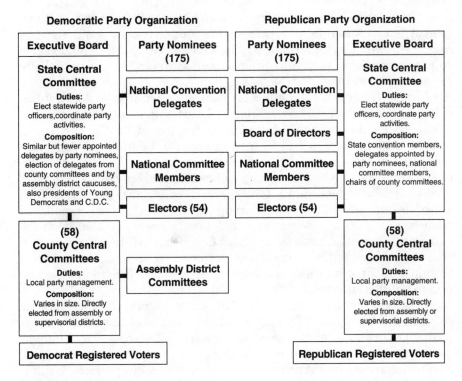

Figure 6.1 Political Party Organization.

Source: California Government and Politics Annual.

Action (a Los Angeles–based group that has helped elect numerous offi-cials). In general, these internal organizations have only an indirect im-pact on the larger political process.

Perhaps because parties are not very powerful, and because most party activists are unknown and unrecognized, many Californians choose to be active politically without being involved in parties.

Outside Parties: Nonpartisan Political Organizations

Outside the party structure and party-oriented organizations are the mul-titude of *grassroots* groupings which for many people *are* California poli-tics. Perhaps the growing popularity of such groups reflects the historical weakness of parties and the current low profiles of the partisan organiza-tions. Or perhaps the problems that confront Californians daily are best approached through *issue-oriented organizations* with no absolute loy-alty to any party.

For those concerned about environmental protection, groups such as Save Our Coast (based in San Mateo), the Labor/Community Strategy Center (in Los Angeles), the League of Conservation Voters (statewide), and the Group Against Spraying People (Camarillo) are in constant need of volunteers' time, energy, and money. For women seeking greater rep-resentation, the California chapters of the National Women's Political Caucus, the California Abortion Rights Action League, and the Los Angeles–based Fund for a Feminist Majority all raise money and organize volunteers to get women into office as well as to elect men sympathetic to feminist concerns.

African American and Latino activists are often involved in Califor-nia affiliates of the Southern Christian Leadership Conference, the Na-tional Association for the Advancement of Colored People, the South-west Voter Registration and Education Project, the Mexican American Political Association, and the Mexican American Legal Defense and Edu-cation Fund, all of which encourage minority involvement in both elec-toral politics and community issues. Asian Americans, rivaling Latinos as the fastest-growing minority group, derive much of their political clout from the Asian Pacific American Legal Center and the Asian Pa-cific Policy Institute, both in Southern California. All these groups con-cern themselves with the ongoing issues of minorities, including access to employment, education, and housing as well as adequate representa-tion in politics and media.

Other voluntary associations that bring people together include Mothers Against Drunk Driving (MADD), Friends of the Library fund-raising groups, local homeowner and resident associations, and numer-ous ad hoc committees that come together for short-term purposes, such as planting trees or preventing unwanted development projects. Califor-nia's organized historic preservationists battle to protect architectural and cultural landmarks from demolition while Neighborhood Watch committees, formed by small groups of neighbors in coordination with local police departments, carry out community tasks such as painting out graffiti, reporting abandoned cars, and keeping track of crime. Voluntary groups whose issues become the focus of widespread concern can ultimately create major changes, such as the "three strikes and you're out" laws that exist in part due to the political organizing done by families damaged by violent crime.

Californians in search of the California dream have two clear options: they can "cocoon" into the privacy of their homes and try to block out the social stresses around them, or they can join other concerned people to work toward improvement in the quality of life. Literally hundreds of organizations exist through the volunteer efforts of people who want to make a difference. The only limits on political participation are the time and energy of people who may find that their "voluntary" political participation soon begins to feel "essential." Once the connections between individual problems and the political process are made, participants find it becomes difficult to return to a narrow, nonpolitical life.

Questions to Consider
Using Your Text and Your Own Experiences

1. What are some issues in everyday life that are affected by political decision makers? Discuss the importance of understanding this connection between daily life and politics.

2. How important are political parties? Why is there an increase in people registering "Decline to state" or in a minor party? What other type of organization can people join to express their political concerns?

3. Debate the closed versus the blanket (or "open") primary. Which one is favored by the established political parties? Which do you favor? Why?

Notes

1. David G. Savage, "Nonpartisan Vote Challenge Voided," *Los Angeles Times*, 18 June 1991, p. A3.
2. Chris Collett, "Bye-Bye, GOP. Ta-ta, Dems. California Voters Flee Traditional Parties," *California Government and Politics Annual*, 1994–1995, p. 70.
3. Ray Reynolds, *California the Curious*. Arroyo Grande, CA: Bear Flag Books, 1989, p. 168.
4. County of Los Angeles Election Results 1996, available from http://www.co.la.us/REGREG/nov96/scripts/ad.html-ssi

Chapter 7

Campaigns and Elections

Money is the mother's milk of politics.
> —Jess Unruh, former Speaker of the California Assembly

Public officials are chosen in a two-step process involving both primary and runoff or general elections. Until June 1998, California had a *closed primary* within each party, which means that voters received a ballot based on their party affiliation. The candidates who wanted to become their party's nominee for the general election were listed, and the one with the most votes, or a *plurality,* won the party's nomination. In 1996, voters passed an initiative calling for *blanket* (or *open*) *primaries* in which all candidates appear on one long list and every voter gets the same ballot. The intent of the open primary is to encourage all voters to help select nominees, but the political parties preferred the closed primary because only members of a party could vote for that party's candidate.

A registered voter may run for an office in the primary by filing a declaration of candidacy with the county clerk at least 69 days before the election, paying a filing fee (unless granted an exemption based on inability to pay), and submitting a petition with the signatures of from 20 to 500 registered voters, depending on the office sought. In an open primary race, each party may have numerous candidates listed. The candidate from each party who gets the most votes (*plurality*) becomes that party's nominee. Losing candidates are then expected to support their party's *standard bearer* in November. In a nonpartisan primary, such as county supervisor, if no candidate receives a *majority* (50 percent plus 1), the two with the most votes face one another in a later *runoff election.* Nonpartisan elections are held for city, county, judicial, and education offices. These elections (with the exception of county races) are usually held in odd-numbered years.

In general elections, held on the first Tuesday after the first Monday in November for state and national offices, voters choose from among the various parties' candidates and vote on any *propositions* that have qualified for that ballot. Most voters actually go to the *polls* to vote, but an increasing number take advantage of *absentee ballots* to vote at home and mail their ballots, thus saving the time it may take to vote in person.

California Politicians: See How They Run

It is relatively easy to run for office in California, but to win requires a combination of campaign ingredients difficult to assemble. One of the most important is an "electable" candidate. Because many voters are recent arrivals in the state and many move frequently, a candidate's long-standing community ties and a wide personal acquaintance are not as important here as elsewhere in the nation. Name recognition is important, however, and candidates spend a good deal of time and money to try to imprint their names in the memories of voters. Political dynasties are built when a familiar name becomes an electoral asset, such as the Martinez family (Congressman Matthew is the father of Assembly member Diane) and the Browns (former Governor Pat was the father of former Governor Jerry and former state Treasurer Kathleen). The Fongs are among the most interesting of the political dynasties: March Fong Eu served as secretary of state as a Democrat for 20 years, while her son Matt Fong, an ambitious politician, is a Republican.

Money and Politics: The Vital Link

In part because name recognition is so important, and because it takes a lot of money to create that, California campaigns are now so expensive that one of the greatest dangers to democratic politics is that races are often won by the biggest spenders, not necessarily the best candidates. Until recently, *incumbents* typically had the advantage in terms of finances and name recognition, but both term limits and the recent trend toward extremely wealthy individuals spending millions to create name identification have altered the situation. Open races in which there is no incumbent sometimes result in a more level playing field for candidates; however, wealthy individuals such as Richard Riordan and Al Checchi can buy name recognition by spending enormous sums on media and mailers. Despite their lack of political experience, both men have become major political figures in California.

Both incumbents and *challengers* spend much of their campaign funds on media, especially radio and television ads. Despite pollster Mervin Field's conclusion that TV ads are "not too efficient" as a way to reach voters because so many of the political commercials reach nonvoters, politicians spend enough money on TV ads and campaigns as a whole to cover the costs of some of the most needed services in the state. Between 1976 and 1990, over $860 million was spent on campaigns, including the money spent for both propositions and candidates.[1] Many police officers, teachers, firefighters, and mental health workers in the state would gladly have seen those same hundreds of millions spent on the services they strive to provide, but the courts have ruled that no limits, except voluntary ones, may be placed on campaign expenditures because they are a form of free speech.

In addition to media purchases, campaign costs include political consultants' fees, polling costs, and direct mail to voters. Direct mail has become an intricate business in which experts help candidates mail persuasive literature to *target audiences.* In tight races where *swing voters* may make the difference, one brochure targets Republicans while another appeals to Democrats. Another frequent strategy is to avoid mentioning party affiliation in order to appeal to the many Californians who are registered "Decline to state." Like other Americans, Californians turn out to vote in proportion to the amount of media attention and controversy generated by an election; it is believed that the legal and emotional issues raised by Proposition 187 helped create a larger-than-usual turnout in the 1994 gubernatorial election.

The millions of campaign dollars come from a variety of sources. The Fair Political Practices Commission (FPPC), set up by voters in 1974 through the initiative process, keeps records of donations. The pattern of donations changed briefly with the implementation of Proposition 208, the 1996 campaign reform act, which restricted the donations of political action committees (PACs) to candidates. However, this restriction on donations was soon thrown out by the Courts, and campaign contributions quickly returned to their usual levels. Top campaign spenders include virtually the same list of pressure groups that also lobby Sacramento throughout the year: oil companies, utilities, telecommunications, banks, agribusiness, insurance corporations, doctors, lawyers, labor unions, teachers, and prison guards.

While most campaigning is done with dollars, California voters occasionally get a taste of the more personal campaign styles of the past. During election season, those who are registered to vote may find themselves answering the doorbell to find a campaign staff member or volunteer coming to chat. Occasionally, the candidate actually visits in person; however, only a candidate who is very dedicated or reasonably well-to-do can afford to quit work to campaign on a daily basis. Door-to-door personal efforts are most effective in local races, where even a less well-funded newcomer can defeat an incumbent when the electorate's mood is right.

Elections Without Candidates: Direct Democracy

Our federal system is a *representative democracy* in which voters elect officials to make decisions for them. However, some states also have elements of *direct democracy* in which voters may bypass elected officials to make laws themselves. California's direct democracy was created by the Progressives of the early 1900s as part of their strategy to bring political power back to the people, and Californians have made ample use of this opportunity. California's constitution ensures that the state's voters can make laws, amend the state constitution, repeal laws, or recall their elected officials through the ballot box.

The most commonly used of the three forms of direct democracy is the *initiative.* The *initiative* permits registered voters to place a proposed law, or *statute,* on the ballot through petition signatures equal to 5 percent of the votes cast in the last election for governor. Amendments to the state constitution require 8 percent. Petition circulators are given 150 days in which to gather signatures. At that time, the secretary of state receives the petitions and evaluates whether enough valid signatures have been collected. If there are enough signatures, the measure is given a proposition number and can be approved by a simple majority in the next election. Due to the high costs of qualifying an initiative and promoting its passage, the large majority of initiatives on the ballot are written and promoted by organized special interest groups, which often pay professional signature gatherers to qualify propositions to appear on the ballot.

Less frequently used are *referendums*, of which there are two types. One type allows voters to repeal a law passed by the legislature. Due to the requirement that all signatures must be gathered within 90 days of the legislation's passage, this type of referendum has rarely appeared on the ballot. The second type of referendum is submitted to the voters by the legislature rather than by petition. The state constitution requires that all legislative efforts to borrow money by the sale of bonds, as well as all constitutional amendments proposed by the legislature, be approved by the voters. In some cases, the legislature places a referendum on the ballot that amends a constitutional initiative passed by voters previously.

The third component of direct democracy is the *recall.* It is a device by which voters can petition for a special election to remove an official from office before his or her term has expired. The threat of recall is more common than its actual usage, and the threat can sometimes cause a politician to change positions on an issue or even to resign. A recall petition normally requires the signatures of 12 to 25 percent of those who voted in the last election; if that requirement is met, opposing candidates may file for places on the ballot. Voters must then vote on whether or not to recall the official and on which of the other candidates to elect to fill the possible vacancy. When voters are really furious, they can unseat an entire elected body at once. In Covina, all five council members were ousted because of voter unhappiness over a utility tax that council members imposed in response to a large city deficit.[2]

Direct Democracy: Pros and Cons

The Progressives intended the initiative, referendum, and recall to be methods by which citizens could make policy directly or remove incompetent officials, thus counteracting the corruption of state or local officials who might be too subservient to powerful special interests. Instead, those same special interests have grown sophisticated in their use of these mechanisms to achieve their goals. Since the signatures of about 380,000 registered voters are necessary to place a statutory initiative on the ballot (and over 600,000 are required for a constitutional amendment), and because signature gatherers must get twice as many as required in order to offset the many invalid signatures found by the secretary of state, it can easily require nearly $1 million just to qualify a measure. Costs to publicize the measure (by those favoring and those opposing it) can go into the multimillion dollar range—just for one controversial proposition. Other problems are the number of propositions that must be read, evaluated, and voted on by citizens who often become disgusted with the time and effort required to do their civic duty. (See Table 7.1.) Yet another problem with initiatives is that measures may pass by large margins yet still have unconstitutional elements that the courts then negate. Critics suggest that the recall, too, is less than ideal because it can be used unfairly against a competent but unpopular official.

Most political experts and politicians believe that California's direct democracy needs reform. Ideas for improvement include having a legal

Table 7.1

Propositions November 1996

Propositions	"Yes" Votes	Percent	"No" Votes	Percent
204 Water Bond	6,019,951	62.9	3,560,084	37.1
205 Jail Bond	3,834,745	40.6	5,606,214	59.4
206 Veterans' Bond	4,993,677	53.6	4,330,354	46.4
207 Frivolous lawsuits	3,206,350	34.2	6,163,645	65.8
208 Common Cause Limit	5,716,349	61.3	3,612,813	38.7
209 California Civil Rights Initiative	5,268,462	54.6	4,388,733	45.4
210 Minimum wage	5,937,569	61.5	3,724,598	38.5
211 Security fraud	2,414,216	25.6	6,997,003	74.4
212 CalPIRG limit	4,539,403	49.1	4,694,166	50.9
213 Uninsured drivers	7,278,167	76.9	2,194,380	23.1
214 Health care regulation	3,886,699	42.0	5,358,331	58.0
215 Marijuana	5,382,915	55.6	4,301,960	44.4
216 Health Regulation-Fees	3,540,845	38.7	5,593,589	61.3
217 Top tax bracket	4,575,550	49.2	4,723,873	50.8
218 Property tax limit	5,202,429	56.6	3,996,702	43.4

Source: California Secretary of State, available from
http://Vote96.ss.ca.gov/Vote96/html/vote/prop/page.961218083528.html

review of propositions before they are circulated for signatures, changing the time limits for signature gathering, enforcing the weak laws that require signature gatherers to live in California, making it easier for the legislature to amend initiatives without returning them to the voters, and enforcing the requirement that initiatives deal with only one subject.

Perhaps one reason reform is so difficult is that the direct democracy process still serves one function: to remove power from elected officials and grant that power to the voters. In some sense, direct democracy adds a fourth element to the checks and balances of the three branches of government, one in which the voters themselves find a voice—a voice that may differ enormously from the ones emanating from the halls of government in California.

Cleaning Up Politics: Campaign Reform

Every few years it seems that there is yet another campaign reform initiative on the California ballot. Often, there are two conflicting initiatives dealing with the same issue. Over time, voters have approved restrictions on transfers of funds between candidates, required reporting of donations to the Fair Political Practices Commission (created by the 1974 Political Reform Act), and imposed strict limits on the amount a lobbyist can spend to "wine and dine" an elected official. Yet it seems that each time voters say "yes" to a reform, unintended consequences of the law appear in later years and demonstrate the difficulty of separating money from politics. In California, thus far, no law has yet made it possible to run campaigns without large sums of money, and no law that limits campaign expenses has been found constitutional.

The Changing Electorate: Who Votes and Who Doesn't

Because about one-fourth of the state's population has migrated from other nations,[3] California's pool of eligible voters is proportionately small. However, recent political pressures have created a sense of urgency among immigrants to become citizens and voters. Traditionally, voter turnout in California is similar to that in other states: Many fewer people vote than are eligible. It remains to be seen whether the new citizens will be dedicated voters and increase the general rate of participation. Nonvoters include the "contented apathetics" who just aren't interested in politics because they see no need to be, people who are devoting all their time to economic survival and don't have time or energy to become informed citizens, and those who are "politically alienated" and believe their vote makes no difference.[4] Voters tend to be affluent, educated, and older than average, leaving many younger, poorer, and less educated Californians underrepresented in the electoral process. Until ethnic minorities and lower-income citizens vote in larger numbers, the trend toward a multicultural state with a *monocultural electorate* will continue. Perhaps the ray of hope for the growing ethnic communities is that new citizens appear to be taking their franchise seriously, with Latino turnout noticeably improving since the 1996 elections.[5]

Having a real democracy requires time and energy from ordinary citizens. Otherwise, the few that bother to vote will exercise disproportionate power, and those they elect may feel responsible to fewer people rather than to society as a whole.

Questions to Consider
Using Your Text and Your Own Experiences

1. Discuss the relationship between money and politics. What forms of power are available to average citizens who do not have large sums to give to candidates or PACs?

2. Debate the pros and cons of our direct democracy choices. Would California be better off without them or with a modified version?

3. Take a class survey. Pair up voters with nonvoters to discuss the issue of voter participation. Does your classroom reflect the monocultural electorate or a changing electorate? Can voters persuade nonvoters to use their franchise?

Notes

1. California Fair Political Practices Commission, *Overview of Campaign Finances: 1976–1990*, February 1992.
2. Andrew LePage, "Voters Angry over Tax Oust Board," *Los Angeles Times*, 14 July 1993, p. B1.
3. U.S. Census Bureau.
4. Richard Zeiger, quoting Mervin Field, "Few Citizens Make Decisions for Everyone," *California Journal*, November 1990, p. 519.
5. Ted Rohrlich, "Record Percentage of Latinos Turn Out to Vote, Exit Poll Finds," *Los Angeles Times*, 9 April 1997, p. A1.

Chapter 8

The California Legislature

*I came up here to be a legislator, which I thought was like being an intellectual
in action. What I found was I was an assembly worker in a bill factory.*
— Senator Tom Hayden (D–Santa Monica)

The California legislative branch is a bicameral body consisting of a 40-member Senate elected for four-year terms and an 80-member Assembly elected for two-year terms. Half the senators and all the Assembly members are elected in November of even-numbered years.

Each Senate district must be equal in population to all other Senate districts, with the same rule holding for all Assembly districts. Thus, each Senate district includes twice as many residents as each Assembly district, and state senators are considered to be more powerful than Assembly members.

The State of the Legislature: Chaos in Motion?

Like many political bodies in the United States, California's legislature is the subject of concern and even mistrust among the public. Periodic scandals in which legislators are found guilty of political corruption get far more media coverage than the dull but essential work done by most others.[1] Battles between the Republican and Democratic *caucuses* or between the legislature and governor also get publicity if the matter is viewed as worthy of media attention, and this bickering and backbiting among public officials no doubt adds to the public's disdain for politics. Meanwhile, California's legislators have the nation's best pay and benefit packages, including steady raises (salaries are $99,000 per year) and generous expense accounts. The independent citizen's commission that approved a 37 percent raise several years ago stated that higher salaries were needed to "attract qualified candidates."[2] Perhaps it is no wonder that furious voters approved Proposition 140 in 1990, which called for term limits for legislators and executive-branch officials.

However, voters may not have realized the full impact of their decision on term limits. Along with the six-year limit on Assembly service and the eight-year limit for the Senate, the proposition cut legislative budgets in ways that led to the loss of many highly skilled legislative staff members. In addition to the loss of experience of these personnel, term limits also lead to rapid turnover among legislators, which simply means more "rookies" are creating our state's laws. A few longtime legislators, desperate to remain in office, have taken to moving to new districts so they can run again after reaching their term limit (the limits apply to a particular legislative district). Despite all these shortcomings, Proposition 140 has brought new faces to Sacramento and may produce a more creative legislature, aware of its limited time. Thus far, the courts have upheld most of the term limit initiative, with the exception of the lifetime ban on running for the same office.

Redistricting and Gerrymandering: Drawing the Lines

Because legislators run from specific, numbered districts (80 Assembly and 40 state Senate), the composition of each district is of critical importance to legislators. In order to keep population equal in legislative districts, the boundaries are redrawn every ten years (normally the year following each census) in a process known as *redistricting*. Lines for the state Assembly and Senate are drawn by the legislators themselves. (See Figure 8.1.) The legislature also has the responsibility to redraw California's congressional districts. Redistricting may involve a manipulation of boundaries (known as *gerrymandering*) to benefit particular individuals or groups or to increase the strength of whichever party has a majority in the legislature. Gerrymandering is highly political, with legislative committees devoting enormous time to partisan battling over district lines.

As the next census year approaches, the two major parties intensify their battle over gaining and holding majority power in the legislature. Currently, Democrats seem to have the edge, but with term limits and the recent switch to open primaries, voter decisions are less predictable than ever. Whichever party holds legislative power in 2001 will probably have the ability to draw enough *safe districts* to enable that party to retain majority control until 2010. In safe districts, voter registration leans heavily toward one party, and the other major party rarely can win the seat. However, outside the safe districts, most other districts are increasingly *marginal*, which means that outcomes are less predictable.

Legislative Functions and Procedures: How They Do Their Business

Unlike Congress, which has complete legislative power in the national government, the California legislature must share lawmaking authority with the voters through the initiative and referendum processes de-

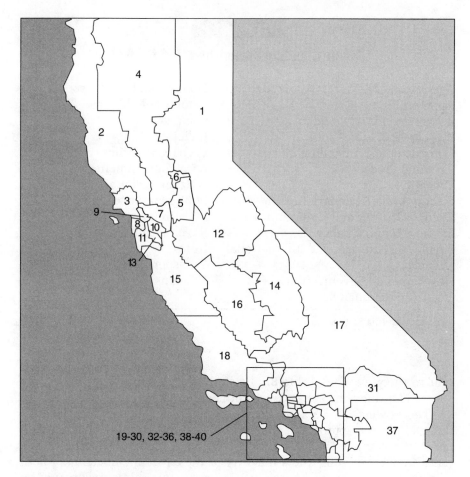

Figure 8.1   Senate Districts.

Source: Senate Committee on Elections and Reappointment.

scribed in Chapter 7. Nonetheless, state government policy is set primarily by the legislature. In addition, it has the "power of the purse," levying taxes and appropriating money to finance the operation of all state agencies. After the passage of Proposition 13 (June 1978), the legislature provided a large percentage of local government revenue as well.

The legislature meets in two-year sessions. A bill introduced during the first year may remain under consideration during the second year without being reintroduced. When a bill is introduced, it moves slowly (with rare exceptions) through a complex process of committee hearings until it reaches the floor of the house where it began. Every bill must go through at least one committee, pass the full house, move through the second house's committee and floor, and then, finally, be

Table 8.1

Senate Standing Committees, 1997–1998

Agriculture and Water Resources
Appropriations
Budget and Fiscal Review
Business and Professions
Constitutional Amendments
Criminal Procedure
Education
Elections and Reapportionment
Energy, Utilities and Communications
Environmental Quality
Finance, Investment and International
    Trade
Governmental Organization
Health and Human Services

Housing and Land Use
Industrial Relations
Insurance
Judiciary
Legislative Ethics
Local Government
Natural Resources and Wildlife
Public Employees and
    Retirement
Revenue and Taxation
Rules
Transportation
Veterans Affairs

Source: California State Senate.

sent to the governor. (Table 8.1 lists standing committees of the state Senate.) During this process, most bills are *amended.*

The powers of the Senate and Assembly are nearly identical, although only the approval of the Senate is needed to confirm certain administrative appointments by the governor. A member of either house can introduce any bill, and a majority of the entire membership of both houses is needed to pass most legislation. A two-thirds majority is required for budget bills, for proposed constitutional amendments, and for urgency measures, which, unlike most laws, take effect immediately rather than on January 1 of the following year. Figure 8.2 shows the procedure followed when a bill is introduced.

Presiding Officers: Each Party Gets Something

The lieutenant governor is the presiding officer, or president, of the Senate. In that capacity, however, he or she has little power and can vote only in cases of a tie. The person with greatest influence in the senate is usually the *president pro tem* ("for a time"), a senator elected as a substitute presiding officer by the entire Senate, and who becomes automatically the chair of the powerful Senate Rules Committee. The president pro tem is almost always a member of the party with a majority of senators. To counterbalance the pro tem's power, the minority caucus selects a minority leader to organize its work.

Like the Senate president pro tem, the *speaker of the Assembly* is elected by the entire body but is typically a member of the majority party. The speaker is supposed to preside over the Assembly but often delegates the actual task to a speaker pro tem while the speaker "works the floor" (walks around lobbying the members). The speaker was once the most powerful legislator, but the speaker's role has diminished because term limits make longevity in this role impossible. However, both the Senate president pro tem and the speaker of the Assembly are part of the "Big Five" who meet with the governor to try to resolve deadlocked legislation. The other two members of this elite group are the minority leaders of each house; they gain their posts by election from their own caucus.

Initial Steps by Author

Idea
Suggestions for legislation come from citizens, lobbyists, legislators, businesses, governor, and other public or private agencies.

Drafting
Formal copy of bill and brief summary are prepared by the Legislative Counsel.

Introduction
Bill is submitted by Senator or Assembly member, numbered and read for the first time; Rules Committee assigns bill to a committee. Printed. Action in house of origin.

Action in House of Origin

Committee
Once in committee, testimony is taken from author, proponents, and opponents. Bills can be passed, amended, held (killed), referred to another committee, or sent to interim study. Bills with a fiscal impact are referred to Appropriations Committee (Senate) and Ways and Means (Assembly).

Second Reading
Bills that pass out of committee are read a second time and placed on file for debate.

Floor Debate and Vote
Bills are read a third time and debated. A rollcall vote follows. For ordinary bills, a majority is needed to pass. For urgency bills and appropriation measures, a two-thirds majority is needed. Any member may seek reconsideration and another vote. If passed, the bill is sent to the second house.

(continued)

Figure 8.2   How a Bill Becomes Law in California.

Source: Los Angeles County Almanac, 1991.

Disposition in Second House

Reading
Bill is read for the first time and referred to a committee by the Assembly or Senate Rules Committee.

Committee
Procedures and possible actions are identical to those in the first house.

Second Reading
If approved, the bill is read a second time and placed on the daily file for debate and vote.

Floor Debate and Vote
As in the house of origin, recorded votes are taken after debate. If the bill is passed without having been further amended, it is sent to the governor's desk. (Resolutions are sent to the secretary of state.) If amended in the second house and passed, the measure returns to the house of origin for consideration of amendments.

Resolution of Two-House Differences

Concurrence
The house of origin decides whether to accept the other house's amendments. If approved, the bill is sent to the governor. If rejected, the bill is placed in the hands of a conference committee composed of three senators and three Assembly members.

Conference
If the conferees fail to agree, the bill dies. If the conferees present a recommendation for compromise (called a conference report), both houses vote on the report. If the report is adopted by both, the bill goes to the governor. If either house rejects the report, a second conference committee can be formed.

Role of the Governor

Sign or Veto?
Within 12 days after receiving a bill, the governor can sign it into law, allow it to become law without his signature, or veto it. A vetoed bill returns to the house of origin for possible vote on overriding the veto (requires a two-thirds majority of both houses). Urgency measures become effective immediately after signing. Others usually take effect the following January 1st.

Figure 8.2 (Continued)

Committees: Where the Real Work Gets Done

As in Congress, all members of the legislature serve on at least one *standing committee.* Most members of the Assembly serve on three committees and most senators on four or five. Each bill that is introduced is referred to the appropriate committee and is considered by it in an order usually determined by the chairperson. Most bills that fail to become law are "killed" in committee; those enacted have often been amended in committee before being considered on the floor of the Senate or the Assembly, where they may be further amended.

In marked contrast to the situation in Congress, committee chairs in the state legislature are not determined by seniority and often include members of both parties. In the state Senate, the power to organize committees and appoint their chairs and members is vested in the Rules Committee, made up of the president pro tem and four other senators (two from each caucus). In addition to the Rules Committee, among the most important are the Education, Budget and Fiscal Review, Revenue and Taxation, Judiciary, and Health and Welfare Committees.

In the Assembly, the speaker assigns most committees except for the Rules Committee. Among the most powerful is the Ways and Means Committee, which, like the Senate Budget and Fiscal Review Committee, considers all bills that involve state spending. Other important Assembly committees are the Insurance, Education, Agriculture, and Transportation Committees.

If either house adds an amendment to a bill that is unacceptable to the house that first passed it, a *conference committee* consisting of three senators and three Assembly members attempts to reach a compromise acceptable to both houses. When a bill is finally passed in the same form by both houses, it is sent to the governor for final action.

Loyalties in the Legislature: Party or Public?

The amount of partisanship in the legislature fluctuates. Sometimes internal battles within a party can be more disruptive than the battles between the two parties. Internal Republican battles typically involve differences between the ultraconservative Christian right and the more moderate Republican faction over issues such as abortion, gay rights, and school vouchers. In a similar way, Democratic unity is undermined by the differences between moderates and liberals over welfare reform, environmental issues, and gun control. In addition to these ideological disagreements, individual legislators may make decisions based on personality conflicts, ego issues, or power struggles. Party discipline exists, but is not always the deciding factor when legislators vote.

Although displays of partisan bickering and egotism may cause the public to have mixed feelings about their legislators, the legislature will continue to pass thousands of bills which, if signed by the governor, can affect all Californians. Just a few recent examples include laws to permit breast-feeding in public, to prevent any doctor from referring patients to laboratories in which he or she holds a financial interest, to require proof of auto insurance when renewing a driver's license, to require convicted sex offenders to register on release from custody, to raise cigarette taxes to finance breast cancer research, to increase the marriage license fee to help finance domestic violence prevention programs, and to require children riding bicycles to wear safety helmets.

Questions to Consider
Using Your Text and Your Own Experiences

1. Define "redistricting" and "gerrymander." How do the two concepts relate? Which word is more realistic to describe the process of redrawing political boundaries? Why?

2. What is your impression of California's legislative system? Is it efficient? Is it responsive to the public? If not, why not? How could the legislative process be improved?

3. How have term limits affected California's lawmaking process? Why do most lawmakers oppose term limits? What do you think of term limits, and why?

Notes

1. Paul Jacobs, "Hill Convicted of Extortion in State Capitol Sting Case," *Los Angeles Times*, 17 June 1994, p. A1.
2. Jerry Gillam and Don Morain, "Citizens Panel Grants Legislators a 37% Raise," *Los Angeles Times*, 10 May 1994, p. A1.

Chapter

9

The California Executive

The fact is that people look to the governor to get the job done.
  —Unidentified governor, quoted by Larry Sabato, political scientist

California voters elect eight statewide executive officials, of whom the governor is obviously the most important. The governor acts as the ceremonial head of state, representing it at various formal and informal functions, and has considerable influence over the selection of the chair of his or her party's state central committee. In the total system of checks and balances among the three branches of government, the governor exercises the executive checks. The most important of these is the *veto* power, especially when used on bills appropriating money.

The Veto Power and the Governor's Budget

When the legislature passes a bill, the governor has 12 days in which to veto it by sending it back to the legislature or to sign it into law. If he or she does neither, the bill becomes law automatically. The only time a governor gets more time is when the legislature goes into recess or adjourns and hundreds of bills may arrive in a few days. In this situation, the governor has 30 days to make decisions about bills. Governors vary in their eagerness to veto, and the frequency of the veto depends in part on whether the governor and the legislative majority are from the same party. If the legislative majority is from the other party, the governor may be sent many bills that are sure to be vetoed because of partisan conflicts or ideological differences. Only rarely can the legislature amass the two-thirds vote necessary to *override a veto*, so the governor's veto is a very powerful tool.

Each January the governor must send a budget bill to the legislature providing for the expenditure of specified funds for all government agencies. Although the bill may be frequently amended before it is passed and returned to the governor in June, he or she may then use the *item veto*. This permits the deletion of a particular expenditure entirely or the

57

reduction of its amount, thereby giving the governor major control over state spending.

Other Powers: Practical and Ceremonial

The governor's other checks on the legislative branch include sending messages to suggest new legislation and the authority to call special sessions. One of the more important ceremonial as well as political moments for a governor is the annual "State of the State" speech given before the legislature and other constitutional officers. In this statement, the governor defines California's current situation and proposes legislative themes for the year. Ideas presented here can then be introduced as bills into the Assembly or Senate by the governor's allies in those bodies.

The governor's greatest influence on the judicial branch is the power to begin the careers of most judges by appointment. (See Table 9.1 and the discussion of this procedure in Chapter 10.) In addition, the governor may exercise *executive clemency,* which consists of pardons, commutations (reductions of sentences), and reprieves (postponements of sentences) granted to convicts. For those with past felony records, however, pardons and commutations require the approval of a majority on the state Supreme Court.

Unusual Circumstances: Military and Police Powers

In times of emergency, the governor, as commander in chief of the California National Guard (unless the President has placed it under federal control), may call the guard into active duty. He or she may also direct the highway patrol to bolster local police and sheriff's officers if intervention is needed on a smaller scale. Obviously, most governors prefer not to face natural disasters or human events that require the use of these powers.

Administrative Responsibility: The Power to Give Jobs

The governor enforces state laws through a vast administrative bureaucracy consisting of about fifty departments, most of which are currently grouped within five huge agencies: Business, Transportation and Housing; Health and Welfare; Resources; State and Consumer Services; and Youth and Adult Corrections. The heads of these agencies, in addition to the directors of the Departments of Finance, Food and Agriculture, Industrial Relations, Trade and Commerce, Environmental Protection, and Child Development and Education, constitute the governor's cabinet and are appointed by the governor, subject to Senate confirmation. The finance director is responsible for preparing the entire state budget for submission to the legislature. In keeping with California's tradition of mistrust of political patronage, the governor actually appoints only 1 percent of the total state workforce, with the remaining state employees being

Table 9.1

Checks and Balances: The Governor's Appointments

Vacant Position	Who Must Confirm Governor's Candidate
Judicial: Appeals courts and state Supreme Court	Commission on Judicial Appointments
Judicial: Municipal and superior courts	No one (valid until next scheduled election)
U.S. Senate	No one (valid until next scheduled election)
County supervisor	No one (valid until next scheduled election)
Governor's personal staff	No one
Governor's cabinet	State Senate
Executive departments	State Senate
Boards and commissions	State Senate
Constitutional officers	State Senate and Assembly
Board of Equalization	State Senate and Assembly

civil servants.[1] However, those several hundred appointed jobs are at the highest levels of government and determine the functioning of virtually every state-run operation.

The governor also has the power to appoint members of many administrative boards, four of which are in the field of education. Appointments are made with the concurrence of the state Senate, and appointees are typically political supporters of the governor. Among these are the following positions. (See Figure 9.1.)

1. The Board of Regents that governs the 9 campuses of the University of California. This board consists of 18 members appointed by the governor for 12-year terms, 7 *ex officio* members, and 1 UC student who serves a 1-year term.
2. The Board of Trustees of the 20-campus California State University system. This board is composed of 18 gubernatorial appointees serving 8-year terms and 5 ex officio members.
3. The Board of Governors of the California Community Colleges. This 16-member group (including 1 faculty member) is appointed by the governor for 4-year terms to coordinate the 71 locally controlled community college districts.
4. The State Board of Education. The 10 members of this board are appointed for 4-year terms to make policy for public schools throughout the state on such matters as curriculum and textbook selection.
5. The State Personnel Board. Its 5 members, appointed for 10-year terms, supervise the civil service system encompassing 98 percent of state employees. *(continued)*

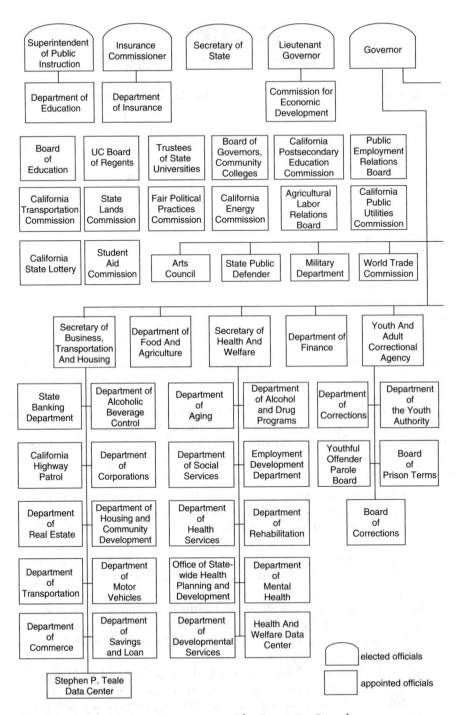

Figure 9.1 California State Government: The Executive Branch.

Source: League of Women Voters.

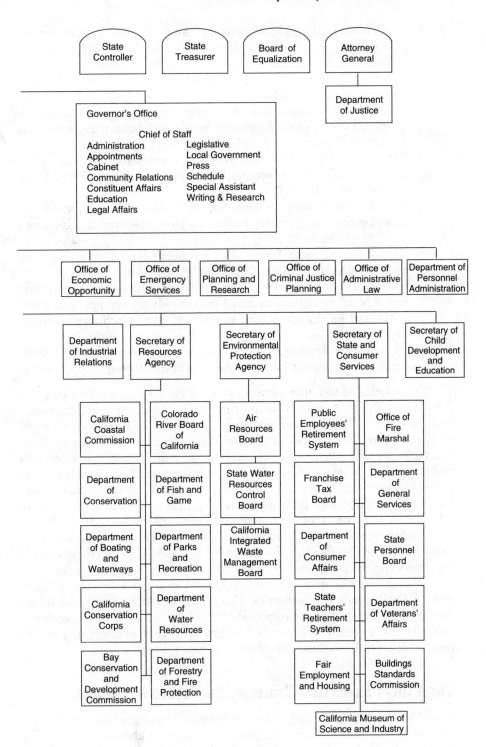

6. The Public Utilities Commission. The PUC, with 5 members appointed for 6-year terms, licenses more than 1,500 privately owned companies and regulates the rates charged and services provided in the gas, water, telephone, telegraph, electricity, and transportation industries.
7. The Energy Commission. Its 5 members are appointed for the purpose of coordinating energy needs and resources as well as promoting conservation and alternative technologies.
8. The Fair Employment and Housing Commission. Its 7 members are responsible for enforcing the laws against both job and housing discrimination.
9. The Workers' Compensation Appeals Board. Its 7 members settle disputes regarding money paid to employees suffering job-related injuries or illness.
10. The Board of Prison Terms. Its 9 members determine which convicts should be granted parole from state prisons.
11. The Public Employment Relations Board. The 5 members of this board regulate collective bargaining involving unions of workers employed by the state government and public schools, colleges, and universities.
12. The Alcohol Beverage Control Board. This 5-member board determines where alcohol licenses can be granted throughout the state.

The politics of the appointment process are well illustrated by Governor Pete Wilson's actions in his first term. He came into office as a moderate Republican and actually nominated some Democrats to high-level positions. Virtually all of his nominees were confirmed by the Senate. Later, as he moved in a more conservative direction and engaged in open political warfare with the Democrat-controlled legislature, he found his nominees being rejected more frequently. In some cases, their rejection was due to an increasing concern that political "friends" were taking positions that should require more relevant credentials.

In addition to the many state boards and commissions the governor must fill, he or she also has the authority to appoint replacements to fill vacancies created by death or resignation on county boards of supervisors as well as those occurring for any of the seven other executive officers and for California's U.S. senators. The governor's many responsibilities are certainly comparable in importance to those of a top corporate executive, yet the governor's salary is $165,000 per year as compared to the multimillion dollar salaries of most corporate leaders.

The Plural Executive: Training for Future Governors

In addition to the governor, seven other executive officials are directly elected by the voters. Like the governor, they are chosen for four-year terms (with a limit of two terms) and hold the following positions, often known as *constitutional offices*.

1. The lieutenant governor, in addition to being nominal president of the state Senate, succeeds to the governorship if that office becomes vacant between elections. The lieutenant governor also serves as acting governor when the governor is out of the state.

   The *office-block ballot,* with its emphasis on voting separately for each state office, has allowed Californians to develop the habit of electing a governor from one party and a lieutenant governor from the other major party. This system, in which the second in command may be from a different party than the governor, has been criticized for promoting inefficiency and poor coordination between public officials. The Constitution Revision Commission has urged that the governor and lieutenant governor run as a team as the President and Vice-President do.[2]

2. The attorney general, the chief legal adviser to all state agencies, is also head of the state Justice Department, which provides assistance to local law enforcement agencies, represents the state in lawsuits, and exercises supervision over the county district attorneys in their prosecution of state criminal defendants. This office is considered a prime position for future gubernatorial candidates, and former Attorney General Dan Lungren used this post well to position himself as the sole Republican candidate for governor in 1998.

3. The controller is concerned with government finance. He or she audits state expenditures, supervises financial restrictions on local governments, and influences state tax collections as a member of the Board of Equalization. Moreover, the controller has considerable patronage power in appointing inheritance tax appraisers and is a member of the State Lands Commission, which oversees the state's 4 million acres of public lands. He or she is also chair of the Franchise Tax Board, which collects income taxes. The office of controller, like that of attorney general, may also serve as a stepping-stone to higher office. Democrat Kathleen Connell, in her first run for public office, became controller in 1994.

4. The California secretary of state maintains official custody over state legal documents, grants charters to business corporations, and administers state election procedures. Among the most important tasks of the secretary of state are verifying the signatures on petitions for ballot initiatives, referendums, and recalls and administering state election laws. Republican Bill Jones, a former Assembly member, holds this post.

5. The state treasurer maintains custody over tax money collected by various state agencies, deposits it in private banks until appropriated by the legislature, sells government bonds (presumably at the lowest possible interest rate), and influences stock investments by the public employee pension funds. This office has been a rotating door lately, with Kathleen Brown and Matt Fong each serving one term before running unsuccessfully for higher office.

6. The most recent addition to the plural executive is the insurance commissioner. Formerly an appointed office, this became an elected position when the voters passed Proposition 103, the auto insurance measure of 1988. The second elected commissioner, Republican Chuck Quackenbush, won office with strong financial support from the insurance industry and a promise to reduce regulation.

7. The six executive officers listed above are, like the governor, nominated and elected through partisan campaigns. The superintendent of public instruction, however, is elected on a nonpartisan basis. The superintendent directs the state Department of Education and is charged with the responsibility of dispensing financial aid to local school districts, granting teaching credentials, and enforcing policies determined by the state Board of Education. In addition, the superintendent is an ex officio member of the UC Board of Regents and the CSU Board of Trustees. Delaine Eastin, a Democrat backed by teacher groups across the state, helped implement class-size reduction for grades K–3.

In addition to the constitutional executive officers just mentioned, California voters choose four members of the Board of Equalization from the four districts into which the state is divided for this purpose. This board collects the sales tax, a major source of state revenue, and equalizes the basis on which local property taxes are assessed by the 58 county assessors in California.

Although the executive branch, including its many agencies, appears large and perhaps excessively layered with bureaucracy, California has been cited as the state with "the most efficient use of bureaucrats" because it employs only 5.75 state workers for every 1,000 Californians.[3]

Despite this positive assessment of the state's bureaucracy, the election of so many executive officials is frequently criticized. The voters have little information about the candidates seeking these offices, and the governor cannot coordinate their activities effectively. This problem is particularly acute when some of the constitutional officers are not in the governor's party or are even potential future rivals for the governorship. However, despite suggestions from the Constitution Revision Commission to reduce the number of elected executive officers (and replace them with appointees),[4] there is little indication that the structure at the top will change soon.

Questions to Consider
Using Your Text and Your Own Experiences

1. Describe some of the governor's powers. Which ones are most important (i.e., which powers affect large numbers of people and are used frequently)? Which ones does a governor prefer not to use?

2. Discuss the governor's powers to appoint other officials. How does this power help shape the everyday lives of Californians? Give specific examples.

3. What is the relationship between the governor and the legislature? What checks and balances are built into the California constitution for these two branches of government?

Notes

1. Bradley Inman, "Many Are Calling But Few Will Be Chosen," *Los Angeles Times*, 17 March 1991, p. D2.
2. California Constitution Revision Commission, *Final Report and Recommendations to the Governor and the Legislature*, 1996, p. 3.
3. Dan Miller, "States' Numbers Say It All," *City and State*, 23 April 1990, p. 14.
4. California Constitution Revision Commission, *Final Report and Recommendations to the Governor and the Legislature*, 1996, p. 18.

Chapter 10

The California Courts

*Our judges are not monks or scientists, but participants in the living stream of
... life, steering the law between the dangers of rigidity on the one hand and of
formlessness on the other.*
                    —Chief Justice Earl Warren, former Governor of California

Unlike the federal system, in which judges are appointed by the President, confirmed by the Senate, and tenured for life with no further review, the state's system involves a complicated combination of appointments and elections for judges. This complex system classifies judges into two categories: lower-court judges and appeals judges. The judges and their courts serve the largest population in the nation; the courts cost approximately $1 billion per year to run and incarcerate about 50,000 criminals per year.[1] They also must adjudicate thousands of civil matters. Although the courts themselves do not create crime or the public's fascination with lawsuits, they bear the burden of these problems. There have been many efforts, including various ballot initiatives, to restructure the courts to cope with the workload and to improve the quality of justice, but any restructuring that does not evaluate the root causes of the courts' burden will not solve the problems for long. Meanwhile, four levels of courts labor with their calendars overflowing and their decisions often subject to debate in the media and among the public at large.

Municipal Courts: At the Local Level

At the lowest level are the 127 municipal courts, with a total of 669 judges earning an annual salary of $98,070 each. Sometimes called *inferior courts*, these tribunals handle such matters as small-claims cases for up to $5,000 in which no attorney is involved and civil suits asking less than $25,000 in damages. In addition, they hear the less important criminal cases (*misdemeanors*) and hold preliminary hearings regarding major crimes (*felonies*). These courts hear approximately 17 million cases per year, the equivalent of about 90 percent of the state's judicial business.[2]

Superior Courts: Each County's Responsibility

Each of California's 58 counties has a superior court, in the larger counties including hundreds of judges. They have appellate jurisdiction enabling them to hear cases from municipal courts on appeal, as well as original jurisdiction over civil cases involving $25,000 or more, felonies, all juvenile cases, and all family law matters. About 790 judges serve on the superior court level, earning $104,262 annually. They are assisted by over 130 commissioners and referees.[3] Superior courts are the major trial courts in California, and, until recently, they have traditionally given about one-third of their time to criminal cases and two-thirds to civil matters.[4] However, because of the "three strikes you're out" constitutional amendment passed by voters in 1994, increasing numbers of criminal trials have taken up much of the time of the superior courts while civil cases have been postponed, sometimes for years.

District Courts of Appeal: If an Error Has Occurred

When an individual believes that a lower court has made a legal error in deciding a case, he or she may appeal—if financial resources are available to do so. California is divided into six court of appeal districts, headquartered in San Francisco, Los Angeles, Sacramento, Fresno, San Jose, and San Diego. Three judges consider each case. The 88 judges each earn $122,893 peer year. The appellate courts tend to rule more frequently for prosecutors than for criminal defendants, but they have no particular pattern of rulings in civil matters.

California Supreme Court: The Last Resort (Almost)

Most of the state Supreme Court's work is handling appeals passed up from the appellate courts. The only cases that come directly to this court are requests from death row prisoners asking the court to review their sentences. The court consists of a chief justice, now Ronald George, receiving $137,463; and six associate justices, who earn $131,085. These salaries are higher than in most other states yet are fairly low when compared with the incomes of the most successful attorneys in private practice. If an individual involved in a case at this level is still not satisfied, he or she may choose to appeal to the U.S. Supreme Court. However, cases that raise constitutional questions appropriate to the U.S. Court are rare, and the state Supreme Court is the final court of appeal for most cases it determines.

The Selection of Judges: A Mix of Politics and Performance

Judges on the municipal and superior courts are chosen by the voters in nonpartisan elections for six-year terms, with no term limits. The basic requirement to become a judge is to have been a lawyer in California for at least five years. The vast majority of incumbent judges are unopposed when they seek reelection, and their names do not even appear on the ballot. However, between elections, vacancies occur because of death, retirement, and the creation of additional judgeships by the legislature. These vacancies permit governors to appoint many new judges to serve until the next election, at which time these incumbents have the advantage. Few municipal or superior court judges begin their careers fighting an election battle; instead, they begin their judicial service through gubernatorial action. Most of them have gained the governor's nomination through a combination of personal connections and campaign support given over the years.

In contrast, appeals court judges and state Supreme Court justices are chosen by a method that requires gubernatorial action before any election is held. The process includes three steps:

1. Appointment by the governor.
2. Approval by the Commission on Judicial Appointments, which consists of a state Supreme Court justice, a district court of appeals justice, and the state attorney general.
3. Election (confirmation) for a 12-year term, with no opposing candidate permitted to run and voters limited to a choice between "yes" and "no." There are no term limits.

In making judicial appointments at all levels (see Figure 10.1), governors usually give special consideration to attorneys who have supported them in their political campaigns and who have a good rating from the State Bar Association. In addition, just as the President can use judicial appointments to promote his or her agenda in the federal system, the political views of the governor have an enormous impact on the types of judges appointed. In one case, Governor Pete Wilson demonstrated his political style by appointing a conservative African American woman, Janice Rogers Brown, who was rated as unqualified by the State Bar. Even though she was the first justice to receive the unqualified rating, she was confirmed by the Commission on Judicial Appointments.[5] Depending on who is governor, judicial appointments generally tend to represent the more privileged groups in society (who have the financial resources to become attorneys and the connections to be nominated by the governor) and do not reflect the ethnic or socioeconomic diversity of the state.

Once appointed and confirmed, few justices have trouble winning confirmation from the voters. With the unusual exception of the "Dump Rose Bird" campaign of the mid-1980s, neither voters nor election strategists have spent much time worrying about who sits on the California courts. Rose Bird, appointed by Democrat Jerry Brown to the state

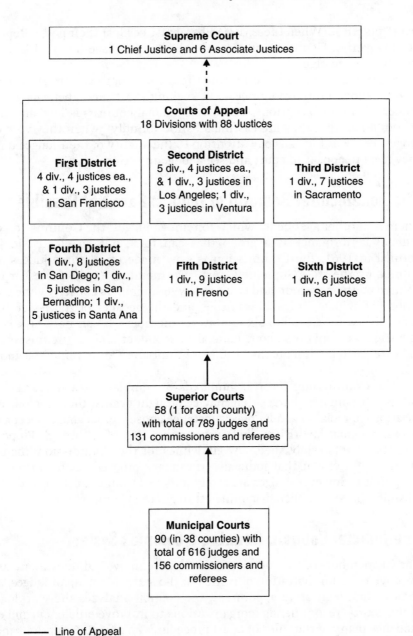

Figure 10.1   California Court System.

Source: League of Women Voters.

Supreme Court despite her lack of judicial experience, became the symbol of "soft" liberalism regarding capital punishment. The successful campaign to unseat her also resulted in the voters' removal of two other justices appointed by Democratic governors, allegedly for also being too "soft" on crime. When these three liberal justices lost their posts, Republican Governor George Deukmejian was able to replace them with three conservative justices.

Since then, voters have returned to a more normal pattern of confirming gubernatorial nominees and keeping most incumbent judges in office. With rare exceptions, interest in judicial contests is low, and voters often feel that they are casting a ballot "blindly" when they vote on judges. Few Californians pay attention to the quality of their judges until they need to appear in court and see a judge in action.

The Nonelectoral Removal of Judges: Rare But Possible

There is another avenue by which to remove judges: the Commission on Judicial Performance is a group that can force out an elected judge. Formed in 1961, the Commission is now made up of three judges appointed by the state Supreme Court, two members of the State Bar appointed by the governor, and two nonlawyer members chosen by the governor, the Senate Rules Committee, and the speaker of the Assembly, respectively, for a total of six nonlawyer members. Its primary task is to investigate complaints about judicial misconduct and, if circumstances indicate, to recommend that the state Supreme Court remove a judge from office.

The Commission receives hundreds of complaints each year about judges. Misconduct charges that may be brought against them include accusations of racial or gender bias, substance abuse, verbal abuse, accepting bribes, personal favoritism, and even senility. In 1994, through Proposition 190, voters established new guidelines for the Commission, including the requirement that judicial performance proceedings be opened to the public.[6] However, judges are rarely removed from the bench, and only a handful have ever been disciplined through the Commission.

The Judicial Council: Running a Complex System

The 21 members of the Judicial Council are empowered to evaluate and improve the administration of justice in the state. Made up of judges, attorneys, and legislative appointees, the council analyzes the workloads of the courts, recommends reorganizations to improve efficiency, and establishes many of the rules of court procedure. Its recommendations may become the basis of legislative decisions to expand or restructure the judicial branch.

Judicial Power: Who Has It and How They Use It

While judges at the local level do not permanently affect questions of constitutionality or set policy through their decisions, the appellate justices and state Supreme Court justices can create legal precedents for

California through their written decisions. Because they wield such power, governors should choose these judges carefully. However, governors have their own political preferences. They realize that a judgeship will probably last much longer than their term as governor, and they select justices whose overall political views are compatible with their own, expecting these justices to make legal decisions that meet their political goals. Of course, over time, some appointees disappoint the governors who put them there by making decisions contrary to the wishes of their "patrons."

Six of the seven current members of the state Supreme Court were appointed by Republican governors. None of the seven ever served as a public defender, civil rights lawyer, labor lawyer, or academic. Most of them come from a background of business-oriented law, and their rulings reflect those biases.[7] With the exception of Justice Stanley Mosk, they are a relatively youthful group and could easily remain on the high court for several decades into the new century. Three of the seven are women, and the court is more ethnically diverse than ever, with Asian American and African American representation. However, they are similar in political views. As it is currently constituted, the state's highest court can be expected to continue on a conservative, pragmatic course for the foreseeable future.

Although individuals who have been in California courtrooms and seen judicial authority in action may feel intimidated or powerless, the public must remember that its electoral choice for governor determines the tone of the judicial branch. If one wants liberal judges, one must elect liberal governors, and the same is true for conservatives. If one wants more women and ethnic minorities represented on the bench, one must evaluate the records and promises of gubernatorial candidates regarding judicial appointments. Likewise, if one believes that justice is color-blind, one must try to elect a candidate who promises to select judges without regard to gender or ethnicity. The important element is the citizen's awareness of the connection between voting for governor and the quality of justice in California.

Questions to Consider

Using Your Text and Your Own Experiences

1. Compare and contrast the federal judicial system with California's judicial branch in terms of how judges are selected, their length of service, and so on.

2. What is the role of the governor in the judicial branch? Does the governor have too much power? How do voters get involved in judicial decision making?

3. Debate the pros and cons of California's judicial confirmation elections. Is judicial independence compromised by this system?

Notes

1. John Berthelsen, "Room at the Inn: Prison Population Growth Slows," *California Journal*, June 1992, pp. 291–294.
2. League of Women Voters, *A Guide to California Government*, 14th ed., 1992, p. 54.
3. Ibid., p. 55.
4. James W. Lamare, *California Politics: Economics, Power, and Policy*, St. Paul: West, 1994, p. 168.
5. "Bar Panel Urges Changes in Judicial Screening Board," *Los Angeles Times*, 19 December 1996, p. A48.
6. League of Women Voters, *State Ballot Measures*, Sacramento, 12 September 1994, p. 7.
7. Bob Egelko, "A Low Profile Court," *California Journal*, June 1994, p. 38.

Chapter

11

Criminal Justice and Civil Law

*We've created 10,000 new jobs in the prison system and financed those jobs by
cutting 10,000 positions out of the university and state college system.*
— Bill Lockyer, former Senate President Pro Tem

All the vast machinery of the judicial system and its related components,
including the judges, attorneys, bailiffs, stenographers, police, jails, war-
dens, and parole officers (to name a few), serves to facilitate two basic
types of legal procedures: civil litigation and criminal prosecutions. Although many Californians' maximum contact with the entire judicial/
legal system is their occasional jury duty, for others their lives are profoundly affected by the structures and processes of the criminal justice
system and/or the civil courts.

Criminal Justice: An Oxymoron?

Depending on the severity of the act, crimes are normally defined as either infractions, misdemeanors, or felonies. *Infractions* are most often
violations of traffic laws. *Misdemeanors* encompass the "less serious"
crimes such as shoplifting and public drunkenness. *Felonies*, the most
serious crimes and potentially punishable by a year or more in state
prison, are tried in superior courts, while the other two categories are
handled by municipal courts.

Although crime rates in the state have gone down in recent years,
Californians continue to show concern about protecting themselves
from criminals. The most publicized change in recent years has been
"three strikes," a constitutional amendment that calls for automatic life
sentences for anyone convicted of a third felony, regardless of the type of
crime. Supporters wanted a tough law, and they believe that Californians
will be safer when "career criminals" are behind bars for life. Critics are
concerned about the costs of providing trials and prison cells for all the
criminals, with current costs at about $3.6 billion per year to house

Table 11.1

California Department of Corrections, 1997

Budget	$3.8 billion
Average yearly cost	$21,470 per inmate
	$2,145 per parolee
Staff	43,068 in institutions, parole, and administration
Facilities	33 state prisons
	38 wilderness area camps
	7 prisoner mother facilities
Inmate population	153,956 (200% of capacity)
	93% male, 7% female
	34% Hispanic, 31% black, 30% white, 6% other
Offense	42% violent crime
	25% property crime
	27% drugs
	6% other
Condemned to death	481

Source: California Department of Corrections, available from
http://www.cdc.state.ca.us/factsht.html

150,000 inmates and a stated need for 17 new prisons in the immediate future.[1] Lobbying hard for more prisons, more staff, and better pay for prison employees is the increasingly powerful California Correctional Peace Officers Association (CCPOA). Table 11.1 lists statistics about the California Department of Corrections.

Crime and Its Victims: Technology Advances, Fears Remain

Even during relative prosperity, California has its share of unemployment, family instability, hopelessness, and ignorance—the underlying causes of much of the crime committed. Despite new technologies such as CAL/GANG, a statewide database of alleged gang members,[2] many understaffed police departments feel they cannot adequately protect the public from thousands of substance abusers, gang members, and street criminals. Ironically, while public fear has increased, the actual crime rate has dropped. With the exception of homicide, most major crimes have declined, according to the attorney general's office.[3] The apparent explanation is the aging of the population, since most crimes are committed by males between 15 and 24 years of age.[4]

Californians in communities plagued by crime have tried everything from forming Neighborhood Watch committees, which try to link neighbors in a network of alert watchfulness, to demanding speed bumps and private gates. Some local governments have responded by initiating "community policing," a system designed to improve communication between neighborhoods and their police forces.[5] Unfortunately, the responsiveness of government agencies sometimes depends on the level of political organization of a community. In low-income areas with little political influence, residents often feel neglected by public safety agencies and do not have the money to purchase alternative sources of protection. More affluent communities have the funds to build gates and walls as well as to hire private security companies to patrol their streets. Ultimately, the amount of crime in a community may depend in part on its socioeconomic level, although the increasing number of violent incidents in suburbs and small towns indicates that no one can buy guaranteed safety. Even the most up-to-date information cannot assure security: For example, recent laws now permit individuals to visit a police station and check a CD-ROM list of registered sex offenders, but early reports suggest that knowing the names and locations of these convicted criminals does not necessarily lead to a greater sense of safety.[6]

Because of immense public fears about violent crime, less attention is paid to some of the more subtle white-collar crimes. Whether the economy is at boom or bust, con artists and hucksters can cause irreparable harm. Californians have been cheated out of millions by pyramid investment schemes, phony mortgage loans, fraudulent land sales, staged auto accidents, and other illegal and unethical ways to part people from their money. While most white-collar crime is nonviolent, sometimes auto insurance scam artists kill innocent people when they create accidents in order to file lawsuits. Victims of white-collar crime are often the elderly, immigrants, and uneducated people.

Even though statistics say that crime is down, the most utilized form of media, television, continues to focus on lurid, violent crime as a mechanism to attract viewers, leaving people with the sense that they could at any moment become victims of random savagery and that political leaders must do something about it. Due to the enormous costs of prison construction and operations, politicians of all views are beginning to wonder whether prevention might be more cost-effective than punishment.[7] The state Department of Corrections has the largest prison-building program in the country. Some politicians have begun to remind the public that it costs taxpayers about $21,500 per year to keep someone in prison,[8] while the state currently spends about $5,144 on a child in public school, $3,000 on a community college student, and $7,400 on a family of three that relies on public assistance (welfare) to survive. Prevention programs could include serious drug rehabilitation opportunities, better use of county jail facilities, job training in prisons, and greater use of electronic monitoring instead of prison time for nonviolent offenders.[9] Figure 11.1 shows where state expenditures are growing.

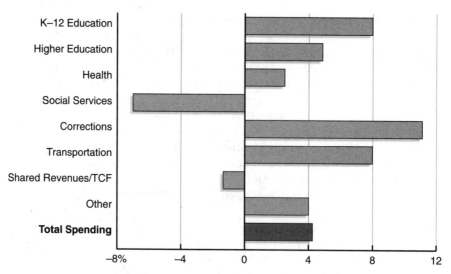

Figure 11.1   Proposed State Spending Growth by Major Program Area.
Source: California Legislative Analyst.

The Criminal Justice Process: A System to Avoid

Many crimes that occur are not reported, and many others are reported but no suspect is arrested. In the cases where an arrest is made, the arresting officer often has the option of "naming" the crime by labeling it either a misdemeanor or a felony. If a person is arrested for a felony, the county district attorney's office must then decide whether to file the felony charge. In cases without witnesses willing to testify, filing charges becomes a dicey proposition in which tax dollars may be spent on a trial only to arrive at an inconclusive outcome. Due to the strength of some gangs, witnesses are often afraid to testify against someone who could take revenge on the witness or a family member.

Prior to 1994, if a crime was very serious and there was adequate evidence for conviction, the case usually resulted in a *plea bargain,* in which the sentence was reduced in exchange for a "deal." This type of deal included pleading guilty to a lesser crime or just pleading guilty in anticipation of a lenient sentence so that a costly trial could be avoided. Plea bargains served the function of cutting down the enormous workloads of the courts, district attorneys, and public defenders. However, since 1994, plea bargains have become less common as a legal strategy, and the number of felony trials has climbed as defendants are advised by public defenders (or private criminal defense attorneys for those with personal resources) to request a trial and try for acquittal rather than bargain for a "strike" against their record. (Figure 11.2 shows where new prisons are being constructed to house the people being sentenced to prison terms.) Trials may be decided by either a judge or a jury, depending

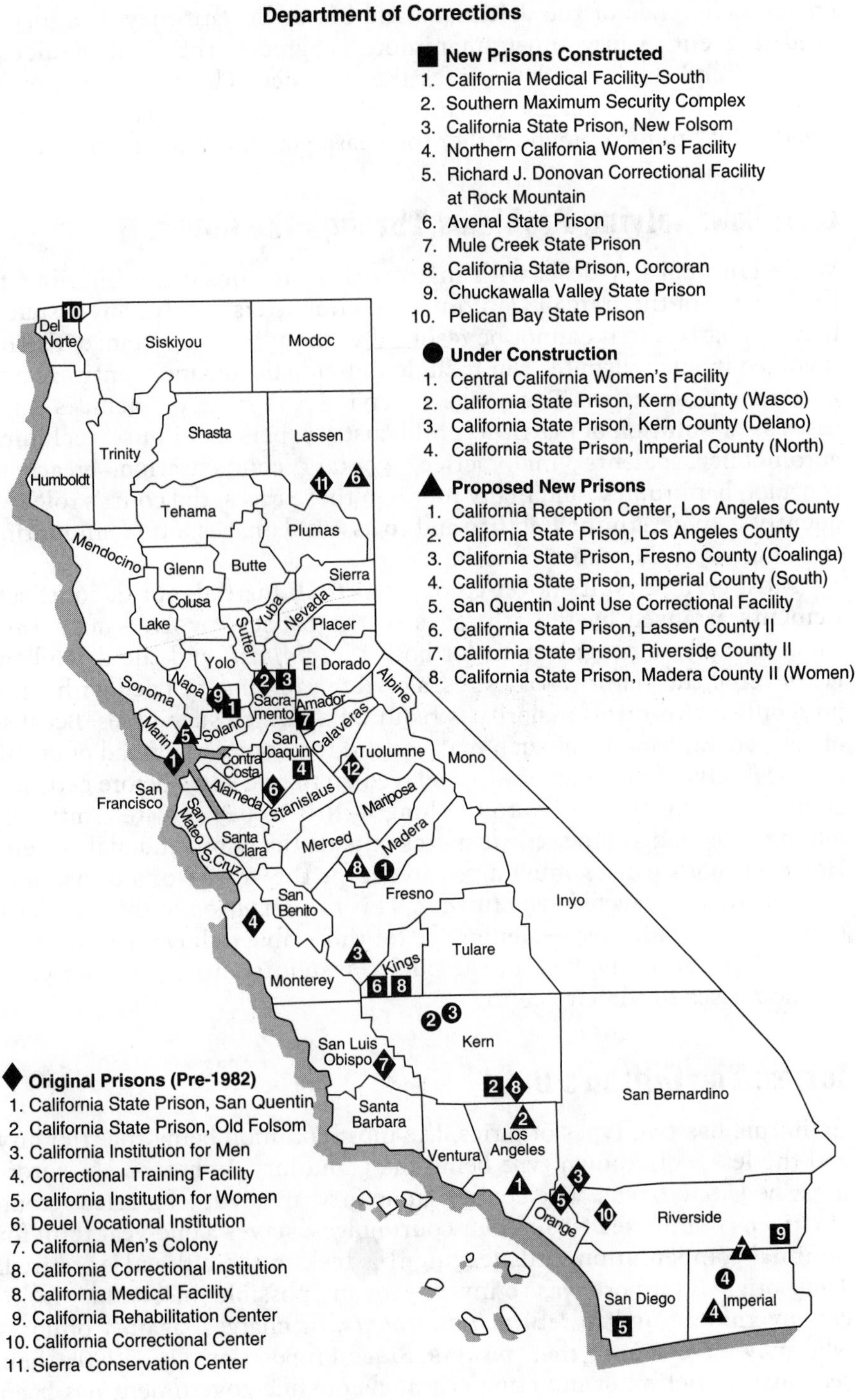

Department of Corrections

■ New Prisons Constructed
1. California Medical Facility–South
2. Southern Maximum Security Complex
3. California State Prison, New Folsom
4. Northern California Women's Facility
5. Richard J. Donovan Correctional Facility at Rock Mountain
6. Avenal State Prison
7. Mule Creek State Prison
8. California State Prison, Corcoran
9. Chuckawalla Valley State Prison
10. Pelican Bay State Prison

● Under Construction
1. Central California Women's Facility
2. California State Prison, Kern County (Wasco)
3. California State Prison, Kern County (Delano)
4. California State Prison, Imperial County (North)

▲ Proposed New Prisons
1. California Reception Center, Los Angeles County
2. California State Prison, Los Angeles County
3. California State Prison, Fresno County (Coalinga)
4. California State Prison, Imperial County (South)
5. San Quentin Joint Use Correctional Facility
6. California State Prison, Lassen County II
7. California State Prison, Riverside County II
8. California State Prison, Madera County II (Women)

◆ Original Prisons (Pre-1982)
1. California State Prison, San Quentin
2. California State Prison, Old Folsom
3. California Institution for Men
4. Correctional Training Facility
5. California Institution for Women
6. Deuel Vocational Institution
7. California Men's Colony
8. California Correctional Institution
8. California Medical Facility
9. California Rehabilitation Center
10. California Correctional Center
11. Sierra Conservation Center

Figure 11.2 California State Prisons.

Source: Department of Corrections.

on the preference of the defendant and his or her attorney. If a jury is used, the entire jury must unanimously agree if the final verdict is "guilty," and the judge determines the sentence. The sole exception to this rule is in capital cases, in which the jury, again by unanimous vote, has the duty to recommend either the death penalty or life in prison.

Civil Law: Solving Problems Through the Courts

While criminal law deals with matters that are considered injurious to the "people of the state of California," civil matters involve any disputes between parties that cannot be resolved without legal assistance. Parties involved in such disputes can include individuals, business entities, and government agencies. The range of civil legal matters includes such cases as dissolution of marriage, child custody, personal injury (including automobile accidents), malpractice, workers' compensation, breach of contract, bankruptcy, and many more. In these cases, the court's role frequently is to determine liability and to assess damages, often amounting to hundreds of thousands of dollars.

Most civil lawsuits never go to a full trial. Instead, out-of-court settlements arranged by the attorneys of the parties involved often save time, money, and aggravation for both the *plaintiff* and the defendant. However, if the plaintiff so desires, a civil matter may be tried with a full jury; only a two-thirds majority is required to decide such cases. Because of the general backlog of such matters and the courts' overload of criminal cases, civil cases may now be delayed up to five years before getting a court date. One alternative to the long wait is to pay private arbitrators (often retired judges) to settle disputes outside the public judicial system. However, both parties must agree to accept the arbitrator's decision or the case will be delayed even further. This *privatization* of the civil legal system may result in speedier justice for those able to buy an arbitrator's time while those involved in the public system continue to wait years for their cases to come to court.

Juries: The Citizen's Duty

California has two types of juries, the most common being the trial jury and the less well known type being the grand jury. In both cases, jurors must be U.S. citizens. The county grand jury, made up of a select group of citizens nominated by superior court judges, serves a one-year term for minimal compensation, thus leaving this task to the affluent or retired. Their original purpose was to investigate any possible misconduct in local government and to return *indictments*, or charges, against officials who may have abused their powers. Since Proposition 115 (1990), their secondary function of indicting criminals outside government has been emphasized to the point that many grand juries have become so busy dealing with criminal matters that they do not have enough time to investigate public officials.[10]

Unlike the grand jury selected for a year, trial juries are created for the length of a particular trial. For felony trials, the jury is composed of 12 citizens, while as few as 9 jurors may try a misdemeanor case or a civil trial. Trial juries are found through both voter registration and motor vehicle license lists. County courts send out notices asking citizens to respond, and those who receive the notices are on the "honor system" to reply. In recent years, penalties for failure to serve have increased, but enforcement is sporadic. Jurors earn only $5 per day for serving, and most working Californians cannot afford to lose their income. Those with reasonable explanations can be excused from jury duty; these legitimate reasons include economic hardship, child-care problems for those with small children, and serious illness.

The jury system has been criticized for many reasons, including the low compensation, which eliminates most working Californians from serving; the potential for emotional (rather than rational) decision making; and the poor use of jurors' time when they do agree to serve. Despite these flaws, the jury system is still considered one of the genuine advantages of living in a democratic society with a constitutional right to "an impartial jury" and "due process of law."[11]

Questions to Consider
Using Your Text and Your Own Experiences

1. What are some of the root causes of our overloaded criminal justice system? What can be done about solving them?

2. What are some alternatives to our overextended civil courts? How else can problems be resolved between individuals or organizations?

3. What could be done to increase the willingness of people to serve on juries? Share your experiences, if any, doing jury duty.

Notes

1. Sigrid Bathen, "The Prison Dilemma," *California Journal*, March 1997, pp. 6–11.
2. Lorenza Muñoz, "Gang Listing Questioned by Rights Groups," *Los Angeles Times*, 14 July 1997, p. A3.
3. Paul Jacobs, "State's Crime Rate Fell in 1993 as Public's Fear Rose," *Los Angeles Times*, 16 March 1994, p. A3.
4. Bathen, ibid., p. 11.
5. Huntington Beach Police Department, "Community Policing," Spring 1994.
6. Patt Morrison, "Now I Know Their Names . . . ," *Los Angeles Times*, 6 July 1997, p. B2.
7. Bathen, ibid.
8. "California Department of Corrections Facts," 1 August 1997, available from http://www.cdc.state.ca.us/factsht.html
9. Rand Research Review, "Focus on Crime and Drug Policy," Spring 1995, vol. 19, no. 1.
10. Bill Boyarsky, "The Watchdog with Scant Time to Watch," *Los Angeles Times*, 11 May 1994, p. B3.
11. Fifth and Sixth Amendments, U.S. Constitution.

Chapter

12

City Governments

The power of local governments to make choices about the level and quality of local services has eroded over the last 20 years. Local communities should be given more local control.

—Constitution Revision Commission, 1996

There are three types of local government in California—counties, cities, and special districts (including school districts)—in addition to regional agencies that attempt to coordinate their policies. Of these, city government is probably the level of local government most accessible to the public. Cities have enormous responsibilities to their residents but are severely constrained by budget limitations, especially the loss of local property tax revenues caused by Proposition 13. As at other levels of government, finding the best ways to generate revenues and provide needed services is an ongoing battle among city officials.

How Cities Are Created: It's Not Easy

With the exception of some of the older cities, such as Los Angeles, San Francisco, and San Jose, which received their charters from the state when California was admitted to the Union, most cities in California "incorporate" when the residents decide they need their own local government. Prior to incorporation, areas that are not cities are called *unincorporated areas,* and their residents normally receive basic services from the county in which they live. Occasionally, an unincorporated area is simply annexed, or joined with, a nearby city by a majority vote of that territory's residents along with the approval of the adjacent city.

Perhaps the most common reason why residents initiate the incorporation process is that the county government that provides their *public sector* services is too far away and unresponsive. If residents feel that police and fire protection are inadequate, or that planning and zoning issues are not well handled, or even that rents are too high in the area, they may organize to create their own city in which they can elect their own officials to control these issues. Of course, residents who want their own city government must realize that there are costs involved in running a city, and they must be prepared to tax themselves to pay for city services. They must also agree to share their tax revenues with the county so it can maintain its countywide services.[1]

Incorporation begins with a petition signed by at least 25 percent of the registered voters in an area. The petition is then submitted to the *Local Agency Formation Commission (LAFCO)*. Each county has a LAFCO to analyze all issues relating to incorporation, boundary changes, and annexations. LAFCO must determine the economic feasibility of a proposed city. If LAFCO decides that cityhood would be financially viable, it authorizes an election in which cityhood can be approved by a simple majority.

In a more recent development, the concept of cities splitting up has become hotly debated, especially in the San Fernando Valley area of Los Angeles. Residents complain of lack of attention and resources from city hall and propose creating a separate city. Legislation has attempted to clarify the process of *secession*, but thus far no city has lost a piece of its territory through this procedure.

City Responsibilities: Many Tasks, Limited Revenues

Whether a city is a "general law" city that derives all its powers from statutes passed by the state legislature or a "charter" city that has its own locally written constitution, all cities share similar tasks and responsibilities. Basic, day-to-day necessities such as sewage and garbage disposal, police and fire protection, libraries, streets and traffic control, recreation and parks facilities, and planning and zoning policy form the backbone of city services. In many cities, some of these services are purchased through contracts with the county to provide law enforcement, fire protection, and street maintenance.

Until 1978, cities obtained about one-fourth of their revenues from local property taxes. After Proposition 13 slashed this source, cities cut back many services and turned to the state capitol in Sacramento for assistance. However, Sacramento does not provide resources comparable to those lost from local property taxes. To fill in the budget gaps, most cities now rely on utility and sales taxes as well as an array of increased fees, including those for building permits, recreational facilities, real estate transfers, garbage collection, and more. Business licenses, parking taxes, traffic fines, and limited federal grants are additional sources of revenue. Since the passage of Proposition 218 (1996), voters are required to authorize many local taxes that have existed for years, and politicians must now make the case for taxes in order to get support at the ballot box. However, because Proposition 218 gives greater voting power to large property owners (even if they are not California residents) and excludes renters from voting, it may yet be modified by the courts.

Despite their relatively diverse funding sources, few cities enjoy the luxury of being able to spend freely, and most city governments spend a great deal of time deciding how best to allocate the scarce resources available. Police departments usually obtain the largest chunk of city monies, leaving fire services, libraries, parks and recreation, and other departments to battle for their share of the pie.

Forms of City Government: Two Basic Types with Variations

Although there are numerous local versions, city government in California falls within two broad types. The *mayor-council* variety entails a separation of powers between the mayor, who has executive responsibility for the functioning of most city departments, and the council, which enacts legislation known as *ordinances*. If the mayor has the power to veto ordinances and to appoint department heads, the government is known as a strong mayor-council variety; if not, it is a weak mayor-council system. Larger cities sometimes include aspects of both the strong and weak systems. (Figure 12.1 shows the city council districts of Los Angeles.)

The *council-manager* type of government gives the city council both executive and legislative power, but the council exercises its executive power by appointing a professionally trained city manager to coordinate and administer city departments. These city managers are usually very well paid (many earn more than the state's governor) and serve as long as the council wishes. In this form of government, there is a ceremonial mayor with no executive powers who is merely one of the council members. This mayoral position is typically rotated around the council with each member serving a year and then returning to regular council status. The mayor continues to hold a vote equal to that of every other member of the city council.

Los Angeles and San Francisco employ the mayor-council form, while Oakland, San Jose, and Torrance are among the 90 percent of all cities in the state that use the council-manager form.[2] Under either system, most cities have a city clerk, attorney, treasurer or controller, and planning commission, with all but the latter elected directly by voters. The most common departments are police, fire, public works, recreation and parks, and building. These are usually headed by high-level civil servants and monitored by advisory commissions appointed by elected officials.

While access to city bureaucracies depends in part on the size of the city, a resident with a complaint about city services had best do his or her homework regarding the structure of city government in order to get the fastest and most helpful response. If the bureaucracy that controls the street-cleaning services is not responsive, the resident with a dirty street must understand which of the elected officials is most directly responsible for that section of the city in order to get the streets cleaned. City employees, while generally hardworking and concerned, may go the extra mile if a city council member makes a special request for a

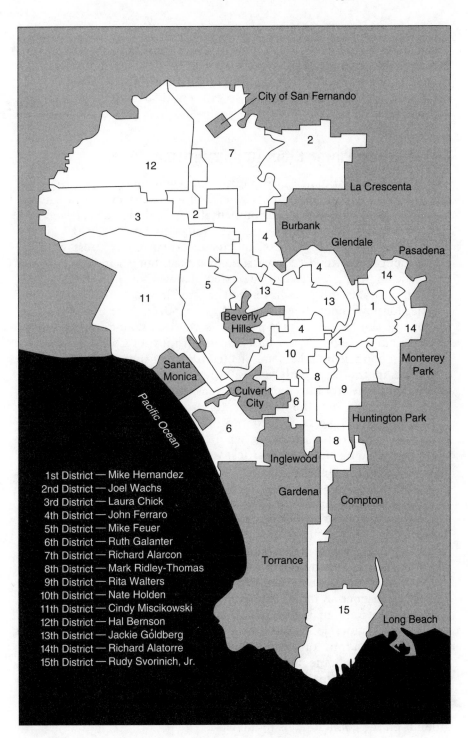

Figure 12.1   Los Angeles City Council Districts, 1995.

Source: City Clerk, Los Angeles.

constituent. Of course, providing service to constituents can sometimes lead to unethical "favors" for constituents. If some constituents receive special consideration, such as permission to build larger buildings than current codes permit, their outraged fellow citizens may demand investigations of elected officials who try to gain political support through this abuse of power.[3]

City Politics: Power Blocs in Competition

The forces that influence city politics are even more varied than the forms of city government. Homeowners, builders, city employee unions, historic preservationists, environmentalists, realtors, street vendors, renters, and landlords are among the groups that vie for clout in the city's decision-making process. In city elections, as in most political races, incumbents tend to have the advantage, but an incumbent who has made enough enemies can be ousted by a well-organized challenger. In recent years, term limits have been enacted in some cities, and opportunities for newcomers have increased.

One of the factors in city politics is whether council members are elected to *at-large* or *district-based* seats. In most of California's nearly 500 cities, council members are elected *at large;* that is, they may live anywhere in the city. Only a few cities use *district-based* elections, which divide the city into geographic areas from which council members are elected. For years, the argument for at-large elections was that the most qualified people could get into office regardless of their address. However, this often meant that whole sections of cities, particularly those inhabited by ethnic minorities, were not represented on the council due to the financial advantages of whites from other areas who ran for office. Since the Watsonville court ruling in 1988, which encouraged ethnic groups to challenge the at-large system if it undermined their political opportunities, several cities have considered switching to district elections. In many such efforts, incumbents have adamantly opposed the change for fear that they would lose their council seats and because of concerns that establishing districts would lead to gerrymanders. In any event, most cities that change from at-large to district-based elections usually experience an increase in ethnic diversity on their councils.

Another factor in how well a council represents city residents is whether the council job is full or part time. In most cities, serving on the city council is a form of community volunteerism with a small stipend paid for countless hours of city-related tasks. In these cases, those able to run and serve as council members tend to be affluent businesspeople or retired persons. In the few cities, such as Los Angeles, that offer a full-time job to council members, the diversity of professions and backgrounds on the council tends to increase.

In between the four-year election cycle, council business is often handled without much public debate or attention. The battle for power that goes on between elections is most likely to be waged at city council meetings, council committee hearings, or planning commission hearings. At these, residents affected by a potential ordinance are empowered to speak to the issues before the decision-making body. The Brown Act, or "open-meeting law," requires that all local government meetings be open to the public except when personnel matters, legal actions, labor negotiations, or property deals are being discussed. Public notice of meetings and their agendas must be made available in advance, although these notices are often tucked away in little-read newspapers. In some cities, cable television offers residents a chance to see their city council in action.

As in all levels of government, city policies are often determined by those who are most able to contribute to campaigns. It is at the city level, however, that well-organized nonaffluent groups can get involved most successfully. Despite fierce opposition from the business community and the mayor, the Los Angeles City Council was sufficiently influenced by a coalition of city workers and antipoverty advocates to pass a vetoproof Living Wage Act in 1997, which mandates that all organizations with city contracts pay their employees a "living" wage higher than the current minimum wage.[4]

Battles over land use and open space are often fought at the city level as developers run into well-organized opposition from environmentalists, homeowners, and public agencies who believe that more buildings will bring increased demands on public services as well as further deterioration of the natural environment. Those who want to build more must increasingly spend large sums for the legal and political battles that surround most major development proposals.

Although many Californians take their city services for granted, the quality of city functions is really determined by the quality of the elected officials and civil servants of any particular city. Disparities in the quality of these services are part of the reason for the vast differentials in property values around our state. A desirable home is a home in a well-run city, and a well-run city is usually one with large numbers of active community members who demand that public officials be accountable to the people.

Questions to Consider

Using Your Text and Your Own Experiences

1. What are the responsibilities of city government? What tax resources can city officials use to accomplish their goals?

2. Compare and contrast the two forms of city government. Which does your city use? What are the pros and cons of each?

3. Discuss the pros and cons of at-large versus district-based city elections. Which does your city use? Which do you think is better?

Notes

1. Frank Messina, "Drives Toward Cityhood Slowed by Revenue Law," *Los Angeles Times*, 15 July 1997, p. A13.
2. Ed Goldman, "Out of the Sandbox: Sacramento City Politics May Go Bigtime," *California Journal*, May 1993, p. 17.
3. Will Rogers, "Intimidation of City Staff is Rampant, Pair Says," *Glendale NewsPress*, 16 July 1997, p. A1.
4. Maryann Mason, "The Living Wage: In the Public Interest?" Chicago Institute on Urban Poverty Paper, 1996.

Chapter

13

Counties, Special Districts, and Regional Agencies

Local government offers a unique opportunity for grass-roots politics because it's a setting where big-money interests can't throw around as much weight.
—Congressman Bernie Sanders, former Mayor of Burlington, VT

Of all governmental units, those at the local level are closest to the people and affect them most personally through such services as public safety, traffic regulation, and the operation of public schools. One might hope, therefore, that they would be the easiest to understand and control. However, because of the large numbers of local governments and their confusing and overlapping jurisdictions, this is not the case. California has a hodgepodge of over 7,000 local governments with a total of more than 15,000 local elected officials who often work to provide services duplicated by an agency a few miles away.[1] It is this chaotic approach to local governance that allows for much "local control" but much confusion and overlapping as well.

Counties: Misunderstood But Vital Entities

California's 58 counties are administrative subdivisions of the state and run the gamut in both geographic size and population. Los Angeles County, with close to 9 million residents, is the most populous in the nation. San Bernardino County, with its 20,000 square miles, is the largest in area. In contrast, mountainous Alpine County, which borders Nevada near Lake Tahoe, has about 1,300 residents, and San Francisco, the only combined city-county entity in the state, comprises only 49 square miles.

For residents of *unincorporated areas,* counties provide the basic safety services, road repair, libraries, and parks. Counties also dispense another complete set of services to all residents, both those in cities and those in unincorporated regions. These services include administration of welfare programs such as Temporary Assistance to Needy Families (TANF); supervision of foster care and adoptions of abused or neglected children; the maintenance of property ownership, voter registration, and birth and marriage records; the prosecution of felonies; the operation of the superior court system; the provision of health services (including mental health) to the uninsured; and control of public health problems such as highly contagious diseases and outbreaks of food poisoning.

In order to adequately provide these varied services, counties must receive financial support from the state and federal governments. Nationwide welfare programs such as TANF receive substantial funds from the federal government, while the state provides a large measure of funding for county health care programs and for public protection agencies such as courts, district attorneys' offices, and county jails. Like the cities, counties have become heavily dependent on Sacramento since Proposition 13. As the state budget has tightened, county budgets have been cut back, leading some to cut basic services. Merced County's libraries have closed and reopened depending on the flow of private contributions,[2] while Shasta County has closed 7 of its 10 libraries.[3] In an effort to allow services to continue while reducing their budgets, many counties have tried to give away their beaches, parks, or libraries to either the state or cities. However, other jurisdictions often reject the financial and legal responsibility. Meanwhile, in its efforts to keep services intact as tax collections declined, Orange County gambled on Wall Street's high-risk investment strategies and lost when the county's bonds plummeted in value, leading to the nation's largest public bankruptcy and years of legal and financial battles to recover the county's financial stability.

In addition to the constant financial troubles of many counties, jurisdictional problems often occur because cities and counties frequently provide identical services in virtually the same community. County sheriff's departments continue to serve residents of unincorporated areas just blocks from areas served by city police departments. As budgets tighten, pressures for ending the overlaps increase. In some cases, cities have simply shut down their own police or fire departments and asked the county to take over that function for a fee. In other situations, both counties and cities have considered *privatization* of services, a way of contracting with corporations to employ staff without making them government employees. This often involves lower pay and reduced benefits for workers who provide public services. Privatization tends to create strong opposition from public employee organizations and interest groups concerned about the quality of government.

A final problem for counties is the issue of adequate representation. With the exception of San Francisco, with its combined city-county status and its 11-member board of supervisors, all counties are governed by five-member boards of supervisors exercising both legislative and executive powers. In less populated counties, five individuals may be sufficient; in counties such as Los Angeles, five supervisors serving 9 million residents seems clearly insufficient. Despite several efforts to increase the size of the Los Angeles County Board of Supervisors, voters have repeatedly rejected such proposals, primarily fearing greater costs. In addition to electing their supervisors, county voters also usually elect a sheriff, district attorney, and tax assessor.

Special Districts: Doing What Only They Can Do

Special districts, most of which were created before Proposition 13 altered the state's financial structure, provide specific services that no other jurisdiction handles. Special district services include water supplies, street lighting, mosquito abatement, transportation, and air quality control. With thousands of special districts (see Table 13.1), California may take the prize for providing local control of services, but the fiscal consequences are large.[4] Normally, each district performs only one task, yet the agency may have a well-paid staff with travel budgets and "perks." Most special districts are governed by a county board of supervisors or its appointees, while some special district boards are elected by the public.

Special districts range in size from small cemetery districts to the Metropolitan Water District of Southern California, which serves six counties and wields enormous political clout, especially during drought periods when the politics of water distribution becomes most tense. Other large special districts include the Los Angeles County Metropolitan Transit Authority and the Bay Area Rapid Transit District. The many special districts, both large and small, create both confusion and costs for Californians. In response to complaints about expensive bureaucracies, the Constitution Revision Commission has suggested a massive overhaul of special districts,[5] but as yet, no such changes have been implemented.

School Districts: The Most Common Special Districts

Of all the services provided by local governments, the biggest and most expensive is public education. This is the responsibility of more than 1,100 special districts, including approximately 630 elementary school districts, 115 high school districts, 71 community college districts, and 285 unified districts providing both elementary and high school programs. These districts each have elected boards whose members are directly accountable to the voters. Their chief revenue source is the state, with some monies still derived from local property taxes.

California's schools were among the best in the nation until Proposition 13 drastically cut the primary funding source. (See Figure 13.1, p. 91.) For twenty years, the public schools declined in measures such as pupil–teacher ratio, maintenance of school facilities, and number of

Table 13.1

Special District Activities, 1989–1990

Number of Districts	Activity Category
1009	K–12 (including K–8 and 9–12)
890	Water utility
783	Lighting and lighting maintenance
586	Fire protection
577	Waste disposal (enterprise)
450	Streets and roads—construction and maintenance
410	Financing and constructing facilities
297	Recreation and park
260	Cemetery
216	Drainage and drainage maintenance
126	Land reclamation and levee maintenance
116	Resource conservation
97	Flood control and water conservation
79	Hospital
71	Community college
71	Ambulance
70	Pest control
55	Waste disposal (nonenterprise)
53	Transit
49	Police protection
48	Electric
47	Local and regional planning or development
41	Government services
37	Library services
34	Air pollution control
27	Memorial
17	Airport
13	Harbor and port
13	Television translator station facilities
11	Parking
8	Health
4	Animal control
6,565	

Source: State Controller's 1989–90 Annual Report.

computers per student. Finally, due to improved tax revenues and public dissatisfaction, politicians finally invested in public schools by mandating smaller classes for all primary grades (K–3). However, local school boards often have had difficulty implementing class size reduction due to lack of space and a shortage of trained teachers. Compounding the

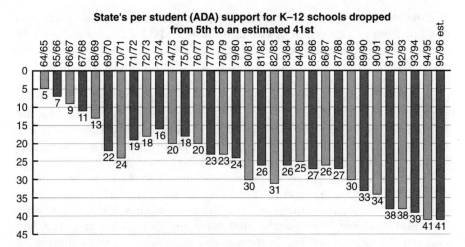

Figure 13.1   California Per Pupil Expenditure Ranking Over Time.
Source: California Department of Education.

overall issue about adequate state funding is the enormous differences in quality between affluent suburban school districts (where property tax revenues are higher) and the schools in most inner cities.

Along with the thousand or so K–12 special districts, 71 community college districts serve the state's adult population. These two-year colleges enable over 1.3 million Californians to earn credits for university transfer, receive vocational training, participate in community volunteerism, or learn English as a second language and other basic skills. There are no entrance requirements other than being 18 years of age (or, in some cases, being approved to attend at a younger age). California residents pay the lowest community college fees in the nation, while students from other nations and states pay tuition that is still considerably lower than that at most private colleges. After several large increases in the early 1990s, fees have stabilized, and California's community colleges still offer an educational bargain for those willing to take advantage of it. Each community college district is managed by a locally elected board of trustees and overseen by a state-level Board of Governors.

Regional Agencies: Two Types, Two Different Functions

The purpose of regional agencies is to coordinate the tasks and plans of all the various local government units in a region. The four largest intergovernmental "councils of government" are the Association of Bay Area Governments (ABAG), including 9 counties and 92 cities in the San Francisco area; the Southern California Association of Governments (SCAG), which embraces 6 counties and 180 cities; the Sacramento Area Council of Governments (SACOG), including 4 counties and part of another, and the San Diego Association of Governments (SANDAG), including all 18 cities and the county itself. These associations study policies on everything from air and water pollution to housing and growth decisions. Unfortunately, these regional agencies are only advisory in nature; their recommendations are not binding on any of their members. Despite enormous efforts to create a Regional Comprehensive Plan to avoid some of the worst problems associated with large numbers of people living in a small area, SCAG has encountered fierce opposition from those who prefer to let each jurisdiction make its own decisions.[6]

Perhaps because of the minimal powers of the multi-issue regional agencies, single-issue regional structures, or large special districts, have developed. Air quality management districts with substantial regulatory powers have been established for Southern California, the San Joaquin Valley, and the San Francisco Bay Area while water supplies for the southern half of the state are handled through the Metropolitan Water District. Transportation in the Bay Area is handled through the Bay Area Rapid Transit District (BART) while the Los Angeles area is served by the Metropolitan Transit District (MTA). Unfortunately, some of these agencies have been plagued with legal and political problems that keep them from performing their duties efficiently, and public concerns about air and water pollution, traffic congestion, and lack of affordable housing are far from being resolved. These problems rarely respect city or county boundaries, yet the current mood of politicians seems to oppose regional problem solving.[7] Perhaps only a regional disaster will bring about the coordination and interdependence that Californians prefer to avoid as they pursue their belief in small government. Like other Americans, Californians value local autonomy and resist empowering larger units of government until insurmountable problems demand it.

Questions to Consider
Using Your Text and Your Own Experiences

1. Describe the responsibilities of counties and their funding base. What are the financial challenges facing California counties?

2. Define special districts and give several examples. Does California need to revise its approach to providing services through special districts? Explain your answer.

3. Why do regional agencies exist? What dilemmas do they encounter as they attempt to create regional solutions to problems?

Notes

1. California Constitution Revision Commission, *Final Report and Recommendations to the Governor and Legislature*, Sacramento, 1996, p. 72.
2. Patt Morrison, "California Dateline," *Los Angeles Times*, 9 December 1994, p. A3.
3. Maria I. LaGanga, "Merced County to Close Its Public Libraries," *Los Angeles Times*, 24 November 1993, p. A3.
4. "Government in California: Buckling Under the Strain," *The Economist*, 13 February 1993, p. 21.
5. California Constitution Revision Commission, p. 74.
6. Al Fuentes (Southern California Association of Governments), interview by author, 30 June 1994.
7. Sherry Bebitch Jeffe, "Southern Exposure: The Decline of Regionalism," *California Journal*, August 1997, p. 11.

Chapter 14

Financing the Golden State

When the economy catches cold, tax revenues get pneumonia.
—Vlae Kershner of the *San Francisco Chronicle*

Perhaps the most persistent problem of all governments is finding adequate financial resources to do the many tasks expected of the *public sector.* Even as people complain incessantly about insufficient levels of service, many of them also fiercely resist being taxed to pay for their improvement. Such contradictions become even more acute in difficult economic times when unemployment rises (thus reducing the total amount of income tax paid) and the needs for unemployment funds or welfare programs increase. In prosperous periods, tax collections may rise, and politicians are tempted to offer tax cuts even if all public services are not fully funded. Whether the economy is booming or in a slump, there are only a few options for government: Raise somebody's taxes, provide fewer services, or borrow money and pay it back (with interest, of course) in the future. Each of these has its own consequences and costs, and it is the process of making these decisions that becomes the annual state budget battle.

How the Budget Is Developed: A Two-Year Process

Every January, the governor must present to the legislature a budget plan reflecting the governor's priorities. This budget requires many months of preparation and input from the executive branch's various departments and agencies, under the supervision of the Department of Finance. The budget is based on "guesstimates" of the amount the state will collect in taxes and *baseline budgets* from each of the state agencies, cities, counties, and special districts that rely on Sacramento as their primary source of funds. Baseline (or "rollover") budgets essentially assume that an agency needs to continue doing everything it currently does as well as receive some cost-of-living adjustment (COLA) raise over the previous year's budget. Of course, agencies may also ask for new funds to provide additional programs, and the governor may wish to initiate new services or reorganize existing programs.

The governor's budget then is examined by the legislative analyst, who reviews and comments on the governor's expenditure requests and revenue projections. Then the legislature begins public hearings held before five subcommittees in each house. During these hearings, government employees at all levels (and their lobbyists) explain why their particular *appropriations* must be maintained or perhaps expanded. Lobbyists for business interests also register their concerns about any tax increases that may negatively affect their industries, and they attempt to obtain support for tax cuts that would reduce their costs.

It is during these budget hearings that the day dreaded by many Californians arrives: April 15. Once tax day is over, the state director of finance knows more clearly how much has been received in personal income taxes and can reevaluate earlier revenue projections to determine whether or not the original budget is accurate. Based on these revised numbers, the governor submits to the legislature the "May revise." If the Assembly and Senate disagree on specific items, a conference committee must be formed to work out the differences. In recent years, the role of the official conference committee has been undermined by the emergence of the "Big Five," a group that includes the governor, the Senate president pro tem, the speaker of the Assembly, and the leaders of the minority party from both houses. The Big Five has become the final deal maker for the budget process, leaving the other 116 legislators the role of rubber-stamping the final agreement.

The final budget agreement is supposed to be complete by June 15 and signed by the governor by June 30. (See Table 14.1.) This rarely occurs on schedule. Due to partisan differences within the legislature and the fact that the budget bill must pass with a two-thirds majority, the struggle over budget choices has caused a late budget nearly every year in recent history. Although a late budget causes severe strains for public services, there is no penalty if elected officials delay the budget. Proposals to streamline the process include allowing the budget to pass with a simple majority rather than two-thirds.

When the budget bill reaches the governor, the chief executive can utilize the *item veto* to reduce appropriations or even eliminate whole programs. The legislature rarely has the two-thirds majority to override specific item vetoes, so the governor ultimately controls state spending.

Sources of Revenue: Never Enough

There are five major sources of money for the state.

1. The general fund, which includes state income tax, sales taxes, bank and corporations taxes, and interest earned by the state on money not currently in use.

Table 14.1

California Budget Process

Executive Branch		Legislative Branch
Administrative departments prepare budgetary requests.	April	
Agencies prepare preliminary program budgets.	May	
Department of Finance and governor issue policy directions.	July August	
Department of Finance reviews agency proposals.	September October	
Commission on State Finance and experts forecast revenues.	November	
Governor finalizes budget and sends it to the state printing office.	January	
January 10: Governor submits budget to legislature.		Fiscal committee chairs introduce governor's proposal as budget bill.
	February	Legislative analyst studies proposed budget; issues *Analysis of Budget Bill* and *Perspectives and Issues.*
	March April	Assembly and Senate budget subcommittees hold public hearings on assigned sections of the budget.
Department of Finance issues revised forecast of revenues and expenditures.	May	Subcommittees complete action on budget.
		Full budget committees hold hearings and vote.
		Assembly and Senate pass respective versions of the budget bill.
	June	Conference committee of 3 Assembly members and 3 senators agree on a compromise budget bill.
		June 15: Legislature submits approved budget to governor.
June 30: Governor exercises item veto and signs budget act.	July	Legislature can restore vetoed items by two-thirds vote in each house.

2. Special funds—including motor vehicle license and registration fees, gasoline taxes, and portions of the sales, cigarette, and horse racing taxes—earmarked for specified purposes.
3. Bond funds requiring voter approval, which are monies borrowed from investors and returned to them with interest in the future.
4. Federal funds, including "free" money and some grants that require matching state or local commitments.
5. Miscellaneous revenues, such as community college fees and contributions to state pension plans.

Controversies over these revenue sources are endless. Which taxes should be raised? Which lowered? Business interests want to reduce any taxes that cut into their profits, while individuals almost always seem to feel that they are paying too much tax. The Republican viewpoint has traditionally insisted on reducing taxes regardless of impacts on programs, while Democrats have often proposed closing loopholes that benefit the wealthy in order to protect low-income residents. Voters must decide whether to support *bond issues* and numerous local assessments, and their record suggests that during hard times they tend not to authorize state spending or borrowing, but during improved economic periods they are more willing to vote for school bonds and other public expenditures. Figures 14.1 and 14.2 show state revenues and expenditures.

Voter Decisions and State Finance: Democracy in Action?

In addition to voting on bond measures, frustrated voters have used ballot initiatives to make fiscal policy for the state. One of the turning points for California's tax policies was Proposition 13 of June 1978, also known as the Jarvis-Gann initiative in recognition of the efforts of landlord Howard Jarvis and his ally Paul Gann to get the initiative on the ballot. Although its passage occurred over two decades ago, the causes and consequences of Proposition 13 are still vital elements in California's situation today.

The roots of Proposition 13 lay in the massive national and international inflation of the early 1970s. While the causes of the inflationary spiral were primarily outside California, including such factors as heavy federal spending in the 1960s and the oil embargo of the early 1970s, these circumstances, added to the traditional speculation in land and property in the state, fueled an enormous rise in the real estate values that determine property taxes. People who had lived in homes for years were suddenly confronted with doubled and tripled *tax assessments* from their county assessors. Fearing that they risked losing their homes if assessments continued to rise, middle- and low-income homeowners gladly joined Jarvis and other major property holders in supporting

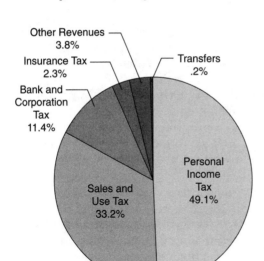

Other Revenues
3.8%

Insurance Tax
2.3%

Bank and
Corporation
Tax
11.4%

Transfers
.2%

Sales and
Use Tax
33.2%

Personal
Income
Tax
49.1%

Figure 14.1 General Fund
Revenues: $52.6 Billion.

Source: Department of Finance.

Proposition 13. When public employees claimed that the proposition
would not only cut property taxes on which local governments relied
heavily but also cut public services, Jarvis replied that "only the fat"
would be cut and that the state budget would rescue counties, cities, and
school districts if necessary.

These arguments were extremely persuasive to the voters. Proposition 13 passed by a landslide, and all property taxes were limited to 1
percent of the assessed value of the property as of 1976, with reassess-
ment to occur only when the property was sold. A budget surplus had ac-
cumulated in Sacramento, so the state did "bail out" the local governments for a while, but many services were cut back, including library
accessibility, fine arts and athletics in the schools, and parks and recreation. Additionally, Proposition 13 had some unforeseen long-term effects, including a shift from local control to a Sacramento-based funding
system for most of the state's cities, counties, and special districts.
There were other flaws in the measure; for example, property owners
who rarely sell (such as commercial property owners) face almost no increase in taxes, whereas owners of individual homes, which are sold
more frequently, confront reassessments up to the current market value,
causing dramatic tax increases. Neighbors in identical homes may pay
vastly differing property taxes based on when they purchased their
homes. This disparity led the U.S. Supreme Court to refer to Proposition
13 as "distasteful and unwise," even as the Court upheld the legality of
the law in a 1991 challenge.

Many observers believe that the reductions in local property taxes
caused by Proposition 13 and the subsequent shift to state-controlled

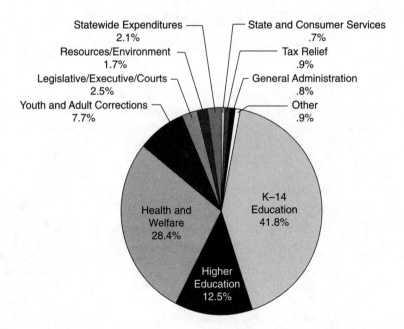

Statewide Expenditures
2.1%

Resources/Environment
1.7%

Legislative/Executive/Courts
2.5%

Youth and Adult Corrections
7.7%

State and Consumer Services
.7%

Tax Relief
.9%

General Administration
.8%

Other
.9%

K–14
Education
41.8%

Health and
Welfare
28.4%

Higher
Education
12.5%

Figure 14.2   General Fund Expenditures: $52.6 Billion. Percentages Based on Budget as Approved by Legislature, Pending Governor's Signature.

Source: Department of Finance.

funding of local government have contributed to the crisis in services experienced in many areas today. Examples abound: County hiking trails charge steep parking and access fees; public school students must sell candy and T-shirts in order to go on educational field trips; many cities charge *user fees* for everything from ambulance services to golf courses and tennis courts. Local governments must go on annual "begging" expeditions to Sacramento, and in recent years, the combined spending of hundreds of local government agencies has become one of the largest lobbying expenditure categories.[1]

Through their ballot activism of the 1970s and 1980s, voters have also placed tight restrictions on the state budget itself. Proposition 98 (1988) requires the state to spend 40 percent of its annual revenue on K–14 education, while another 15 to 20 percent of the budget is set aside to finance bond commitments and voter-mandated programs such as prison construction. Another 25 to 30 percent of the budget is mandated by federal law to provide health and welfare assistance, although federal welfare reform does permit the state somewhat more flexibility in how it administers Temporary Assistance to Needy Families (TANF). Ultimately, the annual budget battle is really a debate about the remaining 15 to 20 percent of the budget pie.[2]

Future Prospects: The Permanent Debate

California and its people suffered greatly during the economic downturn of the early 1990s. Massive job losses in aerospace and defense combined with downsizing and mergers in banking and other industries to create lowered tax revenues. Meanwhile, the newly unemployed needed state programs to retrain as well as income support during difficult times. Reduced revenues and increased demands for government services always create a tense political struggle over state budget priorities.

However, as the state's economy has regained its strength during the second half of the decade, many Californians have seen some improvements in their economic fortunes. Economists predict continued strong growth in entertainment, tourism, trade, agriculture, textiles, and high-tech businesses. But no matter how well some individuals may do, economic growth does not create comfort for all. The state must offer high-quality education at all levels to all its residents, and it must imprison convicted criminals and assist the needy. Even in prosperous times, California still has numerous residents who remain unemployed, undereducated, and/or in poor health. Because of all the demands, state budget battles continue whether the economy is in boom or bust. Perhaps one sign that government can make good use of high revenues during economic booms is the bipartisan decision to spend Proposition 98 funds to reduce class size in the primary grades in California's public schools. In this case, both Democrats and Republicans were strongly supported by public opinion polls showing that voters want their money spent on schools.

Each year as the budget cycle proceeds, hundreds of unique groups demand government support, including schoolchildren and their parents, advocates for open space, prison guards, public employees, library users, college students, welfare (TANF) recipients, automobile users, beachgoers, legal immigrants, the disabled, farmworkers, landowners—the list is endless. For the foreseeable future, California's budget process is bound to be an annual agony that profoundly affects all Californians, yet it is carried out in Sacramento conference rooms far from the scrutiny of television news cameras. Until more Californians pay attention to this process and communicate their preferences to their elected officials, the voices and views of the majority may not be reflected in the budget outcome.

Questions to Consider
Using Your Text and Your Own Experiences

1. How does the general economy affect government budgets? What is the role of government in helping the economy grow?

2. Describe the revenue sources and expense patterns of state government. Who benefits from the current structure? Who loses?

3. Evaluate the budget process through its annual cycle. What are some problems with the process? Should anything be changed?

Notes

1. Secretary of State, *Lobbying Expenditures and the Top 100 Lobbying Firms*, April 1–June 30, 1994, issued September 1994.
2. "Government in California: Buckling Under the Strain," *The Economist*, 13 February 1993, pp. 21–23.

Chapter

15

Issues for the New Century

I am convinced the Big One will persuade Californians to create the kind of deep-rooted communities that can withstand the destruction of the material possessions that have become their Dream's precarious foundation.
—Thurston Clarke, *California Fault*

As the century draws to a close, Californians are finally regaining some of their traditional optimism. Thus far, the "Big One" has not struck despite scientific predictions that a devastating earthquake could occur at any moment.[1] The economy is once again flourishing and bringing rewards to those with the education and drive to take advantage of today's opportunities. Until the next natural disaster strikes, most Californians are able to enjoy their sunshine without fearing sudden, dramatic losses. Nonetheless, the state has many challenges ahead. While some people are enjoying the material success that has often defined the California dream, others continue to experience the dream as a myth. Will the future be best if politicians cut taxes and services so people rely more on themselves or if they tax those who have achieved abundance in order to help the "have-nots"? This perennial question, often representing the poles that divide Republicans from Democrats, continues to face voters and politicians who care about the fate of the Golden State.

The Challenges Ahead: Evolving into the New Century

As the world shrinks due to technological change, California continues to be well positioned for the increasingly global marketplace. Positioned next to Mexico and with busy harbors ready for ships from the Far East, California benefits more than most states from the global economy. Yet the opening of foreign trade through NAFTA and GATT (General Agreement on Trade and Tariffs) has also brought concerns. Should truckers from Mexico be allowed to cross into California to bring Mexican produce and products when those trucks and drivers are not held to American standards of safety? Should *maquiladoras,* or border factories, be allowed to pay poverty-level *peso* wages for work once done by decently paid American workers? "Free trade" is not necessarily "fair trade," and because of California's easy accessibility to Mexico and the Far East, Californians must continue to monitor the ways in which foreign trade affects their living standards.

Along with a strong base in foreign trade, our economy has boomed in both new and renewed industries such as biomedical manufacturing, entertainment, and software production (see Figure 15.1). However, high-paying jobs available in these industries can be gained only by those with specialized skills and training. Those who hire talent for these booming industries continue to complain that the state's poorly funded K–12 educational system does not produce the kind of skilled workers needed.[2] California desperately needs to invest in its educational system, and voters and politicians must make a priority on raising California from 41st place in per-pupil expenditures.[3] Fortunately, there are signs that voter participation is no longer quite as *monocultural* as it once was, and perhaps as the growing ethnic groups participate more in voting, their children will receive a better public education.

Along with the challenges of *globalization* of the economy and preparing Californians for the high-tech future, other concerns that must be addressed include the continually growing gap between rich and poor; the difficulties created by the cultural diversity that also enriches California life; the conflicts involved in managing a complex ecosystem; and the serious question as to whether or not California is "governable."

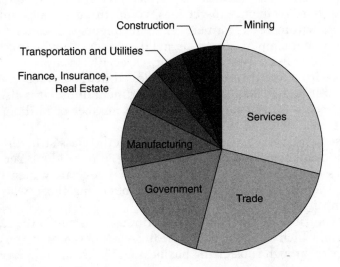

Figure 15.1 Composition of California Nonagricultural Employment by Major Industry Sector.

Source: California Legislative Analyst.

Causes and Consequences: Understanding Today's Situation

In recovering from the deep recession of the early 1990s, California business shifted its reliance on federal military contracts and diversified into
many new areas. However, more than ever, the jobs available in the new
economy are polarized between well-paying careers that require higher
education and low-paying, low-skill jobs. The middle sector of the economy, which once included decently paid manufacturing jobs in union-
ized factories, has mostly disappeared as American industries have
shifted production overseas. This *deindustrialization* leaves behind a
service economy based not on producing goods but on exchanging services, including entertainment, tourism, telecommunications, retail
sales, law, financial services, health care, education, and so forth. In virtually all these service industries, only the highly educated can move
into the upper level while those whose education is inadequate usually
labor for minimum wage or less. This produces a *two-tier economy* that
drastically skews the social and political system. Voter turnout is always
high among the affluent and low among the less educated and lower-
income groups. While the upper class votes, the *underclass* often feels
powerless and neglects to exercise this right.

Perhaps the lack of political action on the part of the poor can be at-
tributed to their daily struggle to survive. Research indicates that the gap
between rich and poor exists not because the rich are getting richer while
the poor remain at the same level but because of "a decline in the income of poor individuals and households."[4] In low-income families, children of working parents rarely have medical insurance; one in six California children lacks medical coverage.[5] With reform policies that
require welfare recipients to get jobs, competition for jobs among the
lower class will increase; former welfare recipients will compete against
over 1 million unemployed persons and thousands of graduating students
seeking work.[6] Being poor is difficult, especially in a place where the
contrasts with affluence are highly visible. While the greater Los Angeles
area has well over 108,000 rat-infested apartment units,[7] it is also an area
that has seen a 38 percent increase in the number of millionaire residents between 1994 and 1997.[8]

These vast gaps are somewhat similar to the class structure in non-
democratic and nonindustrial societies (the "Third World"). Yet the consequences of the continuing income disparity are rarely mentioned by
political leaders, often because they fear offending those who finance
their campaigns.

One contributing factor in this enormous *class gap* is the *regressive*
tax system, which taxes the poor a greater share of their income than the
rich, in part through subsidizing business and longtime property owners
through Proposition 13 and replacing lost property tax revenues with
sales taxes, utilities taxes, and other taxes the poor cannot avoid. Deindustrialization contributes to the class gap, as does the *demilitarization*

that began when the Cold War ended. The hundreds of thousands of jobs lost when the United States decided to reduce its military spending have not yet been fully replaced in the new, diversified California economy. A related concern linked to demilitarization is the trend toward increasing consolidation of what remains of the aerospace industry, which has undergone massive mergers during the last few years as this once booming industry has declined. With each merger come threats of more layoffs of California employees.

As the industrial economy declines, to be replaced by new technology-based industries, human adjustments to these changes continue to involve economic and social stress. While new technology brings new opportunities, it also slams the door on many workers. In the growing service sector, technological developments allow fewer people to provide the same services. Entire occupations are near obsolescence; the work of bank tellers, grocery checkers, and many others can be done by computers. While some service industries must remain in California to meet the needs of their customers, others move portions of their business out of state for the same reasons that manufacturers leave. With increasing avenues of communication, including e-mail, the Internet, and fax machines, many businesses can operate in states or even nations where wages are lower and corporate taxes less burdensome while still serving clients inside California. The service sector of the economy, while growing, often supports low-wage employees such as restaurant servers, hotel room cleaners, and janitors, none of whom earn wages comparable to the skilled blue-collar jobs in steel tires and automobile assembly that used to be readily available in California.

With all of these factors aggravating the gaps between social classes, *scapegoating* becomes more prominent. Fears of competition for economic "goodies" can cause minor prejudices to become full-fledged ethnic rivalries. As more and more Californians are "new neighbors" with different backgrounds and customs, nearly every ethnic group, including the former majority white population, becomes more concerned for its own survival. The passage of Proposition 209, which eliminated affirmative action in all public systems in California, suggests that many California voters (the electorate was over three-fourths white in that election) believe that the "majority" has lost its edge and they don't like that feeling. Demographic data clearly indicate that California's future is multilingual, multicultural, and multiracial. However, due to a variety of historical and social factors, those who currently vote are mostly white and well-to-do. How the gaps between the "old" and "new" California will be closed is not yet known. The challenge is to *acculturate* and assimilate new arrivals without destroying their unique cultural identities and without sacrificing the gains of the American-born population. Part of the solution to this challenge is to provide resources for an outstanding educational system that can help people overcome language barriers, cultural stereotypes, and ethnocentrism as well as teach the technological skills and critical thinking essential for success in today's competitive world.

Cultural diversity can enrich daily life through the mingling of music, food, art, language, and even love (intermarriage between ethnic groups in Los Angeles exceeds 30 percent of couples, the nation's highest rate[9]) or it can be used to divide communities and individuals. During periods when the economy is growing, the need to blame usually is reduced, and calls to block the borders and shut down the safety net are heard less frequently. However, it is in the hard times, when jobs are scarce and government revenues are reduced, that political leaders must show their skill and compassion by emphasizing social unity rather than divisive politics of blame. That ability to show compassion and emphasize social unity may increase as political leaders from diverse backgrounds enter the halls of leadership. One hopeful sign is the substantial increase in Latino political strength as evidenced by the simultaneous election of two Latinos to the legislature's most powerful positions: Antonio Villaraigosa as speaker of the Assembly and Richard Polanco as Senate majority leader. Perhaps that community will set the example for the growing Asian groups. Clearly, all ethnic groups must work toward the common goals of all Californians rather than emphasize an ugly, divisive approach to dealing with problems.

Even as Californians struggle to figure out how to live in the most multicultural state, other problems must not be forgotten. The state's ecosystem continues to require attention even during periods when environmental problems are not in the headlines. Debates over the proper management of California's magnificent natural resources involve numerous special interest groups as well as many concerned individuals. The continuing destruction of agricultural land to meet the housing and shopping needs of a growing population (see Figure 15.2), the unresolved battles over water supplies, the battles over where to dump the inevitable toxic wastes of an economy dependent on chemicals, and the debates over how to clean California's air and water all contribute to the long list of vital issues that must be faced by elected officials and the public. With little publicity, environmental battles are constantly fought. The skirmishes take place in legislative committees, at community meetings, and at environmentally sensitive sites throughout the state. In addition to those mentioned above, issues include how to clean up the beaches and bays, what level of pesticides can be tolerated on our farms and on our food, how ancient forests can be preserved, where virgin land can be developed, and, in general, how to balance the needs of nature with the needs of the over 32 million human beings in the state. Short-term needs for profit and jobs often conflict with long-term needs to preserve irreplaceable natural wonders. California has a large share of nature's spectacular sites; Californians will be struggling to find the right balance for years to come.

Although not every Californian is equally concerned about environmental issues, the long-standing belief that environmentalism is a white, middle-class hobby has been challenged. In fact, it is the underrepre-

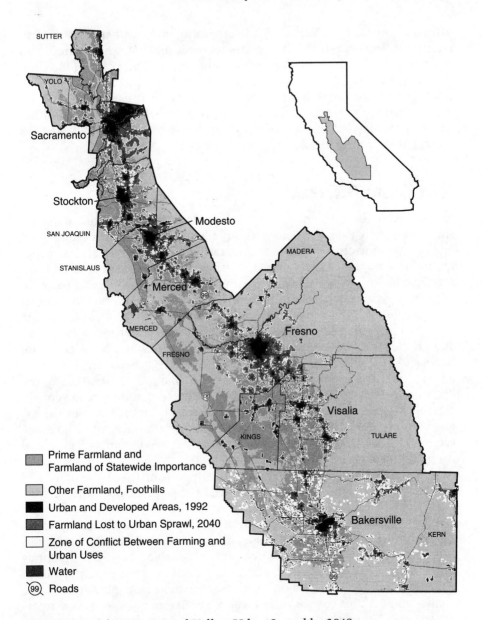

Figure 15.2 California's Central Valley: Urban Sprawl by 2040.

Source: American Farmland Trust, *Alternatives for Future Urban Growth in California's Central Valley.*

sented ethnic groups who often shoulder the burden of environmental damage. Many of the state's toxic waste dumps are located in minority communities, and rates of asthma and other respiratory diseases are worse in inner cities than in suburbs. Environmentally conscious organizations have developed in the African American and Latino communities of South Central Los Angeles as well as in the immigrant Hispanic barrios in the Central Valley. While environmental racism is not a common term, it has come to denote the recognition that ethnic minorities often live in the worst ecological circumstances. The growing environmental concerns in communities of color include questions about lead residues in residential housing, water quality in urban areas, and asbestos abatement in public facilities. Once again, these issues can either unite or divide Californians, perhaps depending on how public leaders present them to the people.

Is California Governable?

Facing such enormous challenges, California needs good political leadership more than ever. Decisions about how to respond to national and global economic changes, how to integrate the increasingly diverse population, how to provide adequate education and other services to all Californians, how to regulate business enough to protect people and their environment yet keep corporations from leaving the state, how to protect irreplaceable natural resources—all of these tasks face a divided state government, which often appears most concerned about its own "perks" and privileges. Divisions abound: within the parties and between them, between the "old-timers" and the "newcomers" in government, and among the many special interest groups that manipulate so much of the decision-making process. To some extent, these conflicts represent inevitable clashes of legitimate yet contradictory perspectives. But the average Californian, trying to earn a living, enjoy a family, and find some security for the future, often appears to have faded from the minds of those in power.

Until all of us recognize the unique opportunities of the state and join with other concerned citizens to right the existing wrongs, it may well be that the Golden State will never again fully reflect the historic "dream." That would be a profound disservice to the Californians of today and those of tomorrow. We can only hope that Californians will pull together to avoid this tragic outcome. Californians of all backgrounds must strive to ensure that all ethnic and cultural groups participate in politics and that all elected officials increase their responsiveness to the public (and perhaps reduce their level of service to narrow special interest groups). No one group can dominate in a state that no longer has a single majority group. It will be the responsibility of the most educated and concerned members of every group to mobilize their friends and associates to join in active, organized efforts to improve life in California.

Unless the general public understands these challenges and their role in them, the future will never be as golden as the state's historic promise. Everyone, to varying degrees, uses the services provided through our state and local governments: airports, highways, beaches, schools, disability checks, community college classes, libraries, driver's licenses, professional licenses, county hospitals—the list is endless. All of us must remember that these services require public money, which must be allocated carefully and spent wisely. Those who protest endlessly about paying their share must remember the part of the American ethic that says, "United we stand, divided we fall." No Californian can be an island; each and every one of us must share the benefits and pay the costs of life in California, the most awesome of states.

Questions to Consider
Using Your Text and Your Own Experiences

1. What are some of the strengths and weaknesses of today's economy? What can state government do to enhance the economic well-being of the state's people? Should government be involved in promoting economic well-being?

2. What are some strengths and weaknesses of California's political and social circumstances? Who benefits and who loses in the current system? How are you affected by this situation?

3. What can you do to make California a better place to live?

Notes

1. Richard Monastersky, "The Overdue Quake: Unusual Activity Along the San Andreas Hints at a Long-expected Tremor," *Science News*, vol. 152, 5 July 1997, p. 8.
2. Hugo Martin, "Funds Ok'd for Study of Job Needs," *Los Angeles Times*, 30 July 1997, p. B3.
3. EdFact Fact Sheet, "California's Rankings, 1995–96," *EdSource: Clarifying Complex Educational Issues*, Palo Alto, April 1997.
4. Deborah Reed, "Income Inequality in California Outpaces U.S.," *Public Affairs Report*, Public Policy Institute of California, September 1996, p. 3.
5. Julie Marquis, "'Shocking' Lack Cited in Child Health Insurance," *Los Angeles Times*, 3 March 1977, p. B1.
6. Doug Smith, Greg Johnson, and Richard O'Reilly, "Aid Recipients Face Battle for Limited Jobs," *Los Angeles Times*, 1 June 1997, p. A1.
7. Hector Tobar, "Riordan Proposes Anti-Slum Plan," *Los Angeles Times*, 29 July 1997, p. B1.
8. "Good Times, Selectively Speaking," *Too Much: A Quarterly Commentary on Capping Excess Income and Wealth*. New York: Council on International and Public Affairs, p. 2.

Appendix A

Directory of Political Organizations

American Civil Liberties Union (civil liberties defense)
1663 Mission St.
San Francisco, CA 94103
www.aclu-sc.org

American Independent Party (conservative minor party)
10997 Seymour St.
Castroville, CA 95012

Anti-Defamation League (antidiscrimination, antibigotry)
7851 Mission Center Court #320
San Diego, CA 92108

Asian Pacific American Legal Center (civil rights)
1010 S. Flower
Los Angeles, CA 90017

California Abortion Rights Action League (pro-choice)
8455 Beverly Blvd., Suite 303
Los Angeles, CA 90048

California Labor Federation, AFL-CIO (labor)
417 Montgomery St. #300
San Francisco, CA 94104

California Public Interest Research Group (CALPIRG) (consumer and
    environmental issues)
1147 S. Robertson Blvd., Suite 203
Los Angeles, CA 90035

California Rural Legal Assistance Fund (legal help in rural areas)
2424 K St.
Sacramento, CA 95816

California Tomorrow (making diversity work, children's issues)
Fort Mason, Bldg. B
San Francisco, CA 94123

Central American Resource Center (CARECEN) (social services)
1636 W. 8th St.
Los Angeles, CA 90057

Chamber of Commerce of California (business association)
1201 K St.
Sacramento, CA 95814

Children Now—California (children's health, education, etc.)
1212 Broadway, Suite 530
Oakland, CA 94612

Coalition Against Police Abuse (police behavior)
2824 S. Western Ave.
Los Angeles, CA 90018

Coalition for Clean Air (air quality)
901 Wilshire Blvd.
Santa Monica, CA 90201

Coalition for Economic Survival (tenants' rights)
1296 N. Fairfax Ave.
West Hollywood, CA 90046

Common Cause (quality of government)
926 J St.
Sacramento, CA 95814

Democratic Party of California (partisan)
911 20th St.
Sacramento, CA 95814

Gay and Lesbian Alliance Against Defamation (monitoring homophobia in
    media)
8455 Beverly Blvd. #305
Los Angeles, CA 90048

Green Party (environmental justice, nonviolence)
P.O. Box 411
Moss Beach, CA 94038

Handgun Control Inc. (gun control lobby)
703 Market St. #1511
San Francisco, CA 94103

Health Access (affordable health care)
942 Market St. #402
San Francisco, CA 94102

JERICHO: A Voice for Justice (social justice)
926 J St.
Sacramento, CA 95814

Japanese American Citizens League (civil rights)
1765 Sutter St.
San Francisco, CA 94115

Labor/Community Strategy Center (environmental issues, social justice)
3780 Wilshire Blvd., Suite 1200
Los Angeles, CA 90010

League of Conservation Voters—California (environmental issues)
965 Mission St., Suite 750
San Francisco, CA 94103

League of Women Voters of California (nonpartisan political reform)
926 J St. #1000
Sacramento, CA 95814
http://ca.lwv.org

Libertarian Party of California (antigovernment minor party)
1800 Market St. #16
San Francisco, CA 94102-6227

Liveable Wage Coalition (decent wages for public employees)
660 Sacramento St. #202
San Francisco, CA 94111

Mexican American Legal Defense and Education Foundation (civil rights)
926 J St.
Sacramento, CA 95814

National Association for the Advancement of Colored People (one of the first
    civil rights groups)
3910 W. Martin Luther King, Jr., Blvd.
Los Angeles, CA 90008

National Organization for Women (women's issues)
926 J St. #523
Sacramento, CA 95814

Peace and Freedom Party (social justice minor party)
422 S. Western Ave. #202
Los Angeles, CA 90020

Planned Parenthood of California (family planning lobby)
2415 K St.
Sacramento, CA 95816

Planning and Conservation League (environmental issues)
926 J St.
Sacramento, CA 95814

Republican Party of California (partisan)
1903 W. Magnolia Blvd.
Burbank, CA 91505

Sierra Club (environmental issues)
923 12th St.
Sacramento, CA 95814

Southern California Library for Social Studies and Research (social movement
    documents, conferences)
6120 S. Vermont Ave.
Los Angeles, CA 90044

Southwest Voter Research/William C. Velasquez Institute (research on Latino
   voting and political action)
1712 W. Beverly Blvd. #201
Montebello, CA 90640

Traditional Values Group (conservative Christian lobby)
1127 11th St.
Sacramento, CA 95814

The Utility Reform Network (TURN) (consumer advocacy)
693 Mission St.
San Francisco, CA 94105

Appendix B

California State Officers

Constitutional Officers

(All area codes 916 unless otherwise noted)

Governor's Office

Pete Wilson (R)
Elected: 1990
Term Limit: 1998
1st Floor State Capitol
Sacramento 95814
445-2841

300 S. Spring St. #16701
Los Angeles 90013
(213) 897-0322

555 California St. #2929
San Francisco 94104
(415) 703-2218

1350 Front St. #6054
San Diego 92101
(619) 525-4641

2550 Mariposa Mall #3042
Fresno 93721
(209) 445-5295

18952 MacArthur Blvd. #440
Irvine 92612
(714) 553-3566

3737 Main St. #201
Riverside 92501
(909) 680-6860

444 N. Capitol St. NW
Washington, DC 20001
(202) 624-5270

Cabinet

George Dunn, Chief of Staff
445-5106

Dean Dunphy, Secretary of Business, Transportation and Housing Agency
323-5401

Marian Bergeson, Secretary of Office of Child Development and Education
323-0611

Peter M. Rooney, Secretary of California EPA
445-3846

Sandra R. Smoley, Secretary of Health and Welfare Agency
654-3345

Douglas P. Wheeler, Secretary of Resources Agency
653-7310

Joanne Corday Kozberg, Secretary of State and Consumer Services Agency
653-2636

Lee Grissom, Secretary of Trade and Commerce Agency
322-3962

Tom Maddock, Interim Secretary of Youth and Adult Correctional Agency
323-6001

Craig Brown, Director of Department of Finance
445-4141

Ann M. Veneman, Secretary of Department of Food and Agriculture
654-0433

John C. Duncan, Acting Director of Department of Industrial Relations
(415) 972-8835

Jay R. Vargas, Secretary of Department of Veterans Affairs
653-2158

Special Offices

Department of Finance
Dir: Craig Brown
http://www.dof.ca.gov
1145 Capitol Building
Sacramento 95814
445-3878

Department of Food and Agriculture
Secy: Ann M. Veneman
http://www.cdfa.ca.gov
1220 N St. #409
Sacramento 95814
654-0433

Department of Industrial Relations
Dir: John C. Duncan
http://www.dir.ca.gov
Box 420603
San Francisco 94142
(415) 972-8835

Department of Veterans Affairs
Secy: Jay R. Vargas
http://www.ns.net/cadva
1227 O St.
Sacramento 95814
653-2573

Office of Administrative Law
Dir: Vacant
http://www.oal.ca.gov
555 Capitol Mall #1290
Sacramento 95814
323-6225

Arts Council
Dir: Barbara Pieper
http://www.cac.ca.gov
1300 I St. #930
Sacramento 95814
322-6555

Office of Criminal Justice Planning
Dir: Ray Johnson
http://www.ocjp.ca.gov
1130 K St. #300
Sacramento 95814
324-9100

Governor's Office of Emergency Services
Dir: Richard Andrews
http://www.oes.ca.gov
2800 Meadowview Rd.
Sacramento 95832
262-1816

Military Department, State of California
Adj Gen: MG Tandy K. Bozeman
9800 Goethe Rd. Box 269101
Sacramento 95826
854-3000

State Public Defender
Dir: Fern M. Laethem
http://www.ospd.ca.gov
801 K St. #1100
Sacramento 95814
322-2676

Lieutenant Governor

Gray Davis (D)
Term Limit: 2002
http://www.ltg.ca.gov
Capitol Building #1114
Sacramento 95814
445-8994

Attorney General

Daniel E. Lungren (R)
Term Limit: 1998
http://caag.state.ca.us
1300 I St.
Sacramento 95814
445-9555

Secretary of State

Bill Jones (R)
Term Limit: 2002
http://www.ss.ca.gov
1500 11th St.
Sacramento 95814
653-7244

Treasurer

Matt Fong (R)
Term Limit: 2002
http://www.treasurer.ca.gov
915 Capitol Mall #110
Sacramento 95814
653-2995

Controller

Kathleen Connell (D)
Term Limit: 2002
http://www.sco.ca.gov
300 Capitol Mall, 18th Flr.
Sacramento 95814
445-3028

State Superintendent of Public Instruction

Delaine Eastin
Term Limit: 2002
http://goldmine.cde.ca.gov/executive/
    exechome.html
721 Capitol Mall
Sacramento 95814
657-4768

Insurance Commissioner

Charles Quackenbush (R)
Term Limit: None
http://www.insurance.ca.gov
300 Capitol Mall #1500
Sacramento 95814
492-3500

State Departments

(All numbers 916 area code unless otherwise noted)

Business, Transportation and Housing Agency

Agency Secy: Dean Dunphy
http://www.bth.ca.gov
980 9th St. #2450
Sacramento 95814
323-5400

Department of Alcoholic Beverage Control
Dir: Jay R. Stroh
http://www.abc.ca.gov
3810 Rosin Ct. #150
Sacramento 95834
263-6900

Department of Corporations
Commissioner: Dale Bonner
Deputy Commissioner: Brian A.
    Thompson
http://www.corp.ca.gov
3700 Wilshire Blvd. 6th Flr.
Los Angeles 90010
(213) 736-2741

Department of Financial Institutions
Commissioner: Conrad W. Hewitt
http://www.dfi.ca.gov
111 Pine St. #1100
San Francisco 94111-5613
(415) 263-8555

California Highway Patrol
Commissioner: D. O. Helmick
http://www.chp.ca.gov
2555 1st Ave.
Sacramento 95818
657-7152

**Department of Housing and
    Community Development**
Dir: Richard E. Mallory
http://housing.hcd.ca.gov
1800 Third St.
Sacramento 95814
445-4775

Department of Motor Vehicles
Dir: Sally Reed
http://www.dmv.ca.gov
2415 1st Ave.
Sacramento 95818
657-6940

Department of Real Estate
Commissioner: Jim Antt Jr.
http://www.dre.cahwnet.gov
2201 Broadway
Sacramento 95818
227-0782

**Department of Transportation/
    Caltrans**
Dir: James W. van Loben Sels
http://www.dot.ca.gov
1120 N St. #1100
Sacramento 95814
654-5267

Office of Child Development
and Education

Secy: Marian Bergeson
1121 L St. #600
Sacramento 95814
323-0611

California Environmental
Protection Agency

Agency Secy: Peter M. Rooney
http://www.calepa.cahwnet.gov
555 Capitol Mall #525
Sacramento 95814
445-3846

Air Resources Board
Chair: John D. Dunlap III
Exec Off: Michael P. Kenny
http://www.arb.ca.gov
2020 L St.
Sacramento 95814
322-2990

**Office of Environmental Health
    Hazard Assessment**
Dir: Joan E. Denton
http://www.calepa.cahwnet.gov/
    oehha
301 Capitol Mall #205
Sacramento 95814
324-7572

Integrated Waste Management Board
Chair: Daniel G. Pennington
Exec Dir: Ralph E. Chandler
http://www.ciwmb.ca.gov
8800 Cal Center Dr.
Sacramento 95826
255-2200

Department of Pesticide Regulation
Dir: James W. Wells
http://www.cdpr.ca.gov
1020 N St. #100
Sacramento 95814-5624
445-4000

**Department of Toxic Substances
    Control**
Dir: Jesse R. Huff
http://www.calepa.cahwnet.gov/dtsc.
    htm
Box 806
Sacramento 95812-0806
322-0504

Water Resources Control Board
Chair: John P. Caffrey
Exec Dir: Walt Pettit
http://www.swrcb.ca.gov
901 P St.
Sacramento 95814
657-2390

Health and Welfare Agency

Agency Secy: Sandra R. Smoley, RN
1600 9th St. #460
Sacramento 95814
654-3454

Department of Aging
Dir: Dixon Arnett
http://www.aging.state.ca.us
1600 K St.
Sacramento 95814
322-5290

Department of Alcohol and Drug Programs
Dir: Andrew M. Mecca
http://www.adp.cahwnet.gov
1700 K St., 5th Flr.
Sacramento 95814
445-1943

Department of Community Services and Development
Dir: Michael J. Micciche
700 N 10th St. #258
Sacramento 95814
322-2940

Emergency Medical Services Authority
Interim Dir: Richard E. Watson
http://www.emsa.cahwnet.gov
1930 9th St.
Sacramento 95814
322-4336

Employment Development Department
Dir: Ray Remy
http://www.edd.cahwnet.gov
800 Capitol Mall #5000
Sacramento 95814
654-8210

Department of Health Services
Dir: S. Kimberly Belshe
http://www.dhs.cahwnet.gov
714 P St. #1253
Sacramento 95814
657-1425

Department of Mental Health
Dir: Stephen W. Mayberg
http://www.dmh.cahwnet.gov
1600 9th St. #151
Sacramento 95814
654-2309

Department of Rehabilitation
Dir: Brenda Premo
http://www.rehab.cahwnet.gov
830 K St. #307
Sacramento 95814
445-3971

Department of Social Services
Dir: Eloise Anderson
http://www.dss.cahwnet.gov
744 P St. #1740
Sacramento 95814
657-3667

Resources Agency

Agency Secy: Douglas P. Wheeler
http://ceres.ca.gov/cra
1416 9th St. #1311
Sacramento 95814
653-5656

California Coastal Commission
Chair: Rusty Arieas
Exec Dir: Peter Douglas
http://www.ceres.ca.gov/
    coastalcomm/web
45 Fremont St. #2000
San Francisco 94105
(415) 904-5200

Colorado River Board of California
Chair: Raymond R. Rummonds
Exec Dir: Gerald R. Zimmerman
770 Fairmont Ave. #100
Glendale 91203-1035
(818) 543-4676

California Conservation Corps
Dir: Al Aramburu
http://www.ccc.ca.gov
1719 24th St.
Sacramento 95814
341-3100

Department of Fish and Game
Dir: Jacqueline E. Schafer
http://www.dfg.ca.gov
1416 9th St., 12th Flr.
Sacramento 95814
653-7664

**Department of Forestry and
    Fire Protection**
Dir: Richard A. Wilson
http://www.fire.ca.gov
1416 9th St. #1505
Sacramento 95814
653-5121

**Department of Parks and
    Recreation**
Dir: Donald W. Murphy
http://www.ceres.ca.gov/parks
1416 9th St. #1405
Sacramento 95814
653-8380

**Santa Monica Mountains
    Conservancy**
Exec Dir: Joseph T. Edmiston
http://www.ceres.ca.gov/smmc
5750 Ramirez Canyon Rd.
Malibu 90265
(310) 589-3200

California Tahoe Conservancy
Exec Off: Dennis Machida
Box 7758
South Lake Tahoe 96158
542-5580

Department of Water Resources
Dir: David N. Kennedy
http://www.water.ca.gov
1416 9th St. #1115-1
Sacramento 95814
653-5791

California Wildlife Foundation
Chair: Michael D. McCollum
Box 18-9577
Sacramento 95818
455-0636

State and Consumer Services Agency

Agency Secy: Joanne Corday Kozberg
915 Capitol Mall #200
Sacramento 95814
653-2636

Department of Consumer Affairs
Dir: Marjorie M. Berte
http://www.dca.ca.gov
2014 T St. #210
Sacramento 95814
227-2873

**Fair Employment and Housing
    Commission**
Chair: Lydia I. Beebe
1390 Market St. #410
San Francisco 94102-5377
(415) 557-2325

California Franchise Tax Board
Chair: Kathleen Connell
http://www.ftb.ca.gov
Box 1468
Sacramento 95812-1468
845-4543

**California Museum of Science
    and Industry**
Exec Dir: Jeffrey N. Rudolph
700 State Dr.
Los Angeles 90037
(213) 744-7400

State Personnel Board
Act Exec Off: Walter Vaughn
http://www.spb.ca.gov
801 Capitol Mall
Sacramento 95814
653-1028

Psychology, Board of
Chair: Bruce Ebert
1422 Howe Ave. #22
Sacramento 95825-3200
263-2699

State Teachers Retirement System
CEO: James Mosman
7667 Folsom Blvd., 3rd Flr.
Sacramento 95826
229-3700

**California Public Employees
    Retirement System (CalPERS)**
Pres: William D. Crist
http://www.calpers.ca.gov
400 P St.
Sacramento 95814
326-3829

Trade and Commerce Agency

Agency Secy: Lee Grissom
http://commerce.ca.gov/index.html
801 K St. #1700
Sacramento 95814
322-1394

California Film Commission
Dir: Patti Stolkin Archuletta
http://commerce.ca.gov/business/
    select/film
7080 Hollywood Blvd. #900
Hollywood 90028
(213) 860-2960

California Division of Tourism
Dir: John Poimiroo
http://www.gocalif.ca.gov
801 K St. #1600
Sacramento 95814
322-2881

**Division of International Trade and
    Investment/World Trade
    Commission**
Act Dpty Secy: Lloyd C. Day
http://commerce.ca.gov/international
801 K St. #1926
Sacramento 95814-3520
324-5511

Youth and Adult Correctional Agency

Act Secy: Tom Maddock
http://www.yaca.state.ca.us
1100 11th St. #400
Sacramento 95814
323-6001

Corrections, Board of
Act Chair: Thomas M. Maddock
http://www.bdcorr.ca.gov
600 Bercut Dr.
Sacramento 95814
445-5073

Department of Corrections
Dir: Cal Terhune
http://www.cdc.state.ca.us
1515 S St.
Sacramento 95814
445-7688

Prison Industry Board
Chair: Cal Terhune
560 E. Natoma St.
Folsom 95630-2200
358-2677

Prison Terms, Board of
Chair: James W. Nielsen
http://www.bpt.ca.gov
428 J St., 6th Flr.
Sacramento 95814
445-4072

Youth Authority
Dir: Francisco J. Alarcon
http://www.cya.ca.gov
4241 Williamsbourgh Dr.
Sacramento 95823
262-1480

Youthful Offender Parole Board
Chair: Robert B. Presley
http://www.yopb.ca.gov
4241 Williamsbourgh Dr. #213
Sacramento 95823
262-1550

California State Senate

(The Capitol address for all members is Sacramento, CA 95814. All area codes 916 unless otherwise noted.)

President, Lt. Gov. Gray Davis (D)
President pro Tempore, John Burton (D)
Democratic Floor Leader, Richard Polanco
Republican Floor Leader, Rob Hurtt
Majority Whip, Leroy Greene (D)
Minority Whip, Ray Haynes (R)
Democratic Caucus Chair, Jack O'Connell
Republican Caucus Chair, Ross Johnson

(Addresses and staff assignments, current as of February 3, 1998, are subject to change.)

Deirdre "Dede" Alpert (D-39)
Term Limit: 2004
senator.alpert@sen.ca.gov
San Diego

Ruben S. Ayala (D-32)
Term Limit: 1998
senator.ayala@sen.ca.gov
Rancho Cucamonga

Jim Brulte (R-31)
Term Limit: 2004
senator.brulte@sen.ca.gov
Rancho Cucamonga

John Burton (D-3)
Term Limit: 2004
San Francisco

Charles Calderon (D-30)
Term Limit: 1998
senator.calderon@sen.ca.gov
Montebello

Jim Costa (D-16)
Term Limit: 2002
Fresno

William A. Craven (R-38)
Term Limit: 1998
Carlsbad

Ralph C. Dills (D-28)
Term Limit: 1998
Gardena

Leroy F. Greene (D-6)
Term Limit: 1998
senator.greene@sen.ca.gov
Sacramento

Tom Hayden (D-23)
Term Limit: 2000
Los Angeles

Ray Haynes (R-36)
Term Limit: 2002
senator.haynes@sen.ca.gov
Riverside

Teresa Hughes (D-25)
Term Limit: 2000
senator.hughes@sen.ca.gov
Inglewood

Rob Hurtt (R-34)
Term Limit: 2002
senator.hurtt@sen.ca.gov
Garden Grove

K. Maurice Johannessen (R-4)
Term Limit: 2002
Redding

Ross Johnson (R-35)
Term Limit: 2004
Irvine

Patrick Johnston (D-5)
Term Limit: 2000
senator.johnston@sen.ca.gov
Stockton

Betty Karnette (D-27)
Term Limit: 2004
senator.karnette@sen.ca.gov
Long Beach

David G. Kelley (R-37)
Term Limit: 2000
senator.kelley@sen.ca.gov
San Diego

William Knight (R-17)
Term Limit: 2004
senator.knight@sen.ca.gov
Palmdale

Quentin L. Kopp (I-8)
Term Limit: 1998
senator.kopp@sen.ca.gov
Daly City

Barbara Lee (D-9)
Term Limit: 2004
senator.lee@sen.ca.gov
Oakland

Tim Leslie (R-1)
Term Limit: 2000
senator.leslie@sen.ca.gov
Roseville

John R. Lewis (R-33)
Term Limit: 2000
senator.lewis@sen.ca.gov
Orange

Bill Lockyer (D-10)
Term Limit: 1998
senator.lockyer@sen.ca.gov
Hayward

Ken Maddy (R-14)
Term Limit: 1998
senator.maddy@sen.ca.gov
Fresno

Bruce McPherson (R-15)
Term Limit: 2004
senator.mcpherson@sen.ca.gov
Santa Cruz

Dick Monteith (R-12)
Term Limit: 2002
senator.monteith@sen.ca.gov
Modesto

Richard L. Mountjoy (R-29)
Term Limit: 2004
senator.mountjoy@sen.ca.gov
Arcadia

Jack O'Connell (D-18)
Term Limit: 2002
senator.oconnell@sen.ca.gov
Santa Barbara

Steve Peace (D-40)
Term Limit: 2002
senator.peace@sen.ca.gov
La Mesa

Richard Polanco (D-22)
Term Limit: 2002
Los Angeles

Richard K. Rainey (R-7)
Term Limit: 2004
senator.rainey@sen.ca.gov
Walnut Creek

Herschel Rosenthal (D-20)
Term Limit: 1998
senator.rosenthal@sen.ca.gov
Van Nuys

Adam Schiff (D-21)
Term Limit: 2004
senator.schiff@sen.ca.gov
Pasadena

Byron D. Sher (D-11)
Term Limit: 2004
senator.sher@sen.ca.gov
Redwood City

Hilda L. Solis (D-24)
Term Limit: 2002
El Monte

Mike Thompson (D-2)
Term Limit: 1998
senator.thompson@sen.ca.gov
Napa

John Vasconcellos (D-13)
Term Limit: 2004
senator.vasconcellos@sen.ca.gov
San Jose

Diane E. Watson (D-26)
Term Limit: 1998
senator.watson@sen.ca.gov
Los Angeles

Cathie Wright (R-19)
Term Limit: 2000
senator.wright@sen.ca.gov
Simi Valley

California State Assembly

(The Capitol address for all members is Sacramento, CA 95814. All area codes 916 unless otherwise noted.)

Speaker, Antonio Villaraigosa (D)
Speaker pro Tempore, Sheila Kuehl (D)
Democratic Floor Leader, Vacant
Republican Floor Leader, Bill Leonard
Democratic Whip, Martha Escutia
Democratic Whip, Michael Sweeney
Republican Whip, George Runner
Republican Whip, Dick Ackerman
Democratic Caucus Chair, Kevin Shelley
Republican Caucus Chair, Lynne Leach

(Addresses and staff assignments, current as of February 3, 1998, are subject to change.)

Dick Ackerman (R-72)
Term Limit: 2000
Fullerton

Fred Aguiar (R-61)
Term Limit: 1998
aguiarft@asm.ca.gov
Ontario

Barbara Alby (R-5)
Term Limit: 1998
barbara.alby@asm.ca.gov
Sacramento

Elaine White Alquist (D-22)
Term Limit: 2002
elaine.alquist@assembly.ca.gov
Santa Clara

Dion Aroner (D-14)
Term Limit: 2002
dion.aroner@assembly.ca.gov
Berkeley

Roy Ashburn (R-32)
Term Limit: 2002
roy.ashburn@assembly.ca.gov
Bakersfield

Joe Baca (D-62)
Term Limit: 1998
joe.baca@assembly.ca.gov
San Bernardino

Steve Baldwin (R-77)
Term Limit: 2000
assemblyman.baldwin@assembly.ca.gov
La Mesa

Jim Battin (R-80)
Term Limit: 2000
jim.battin@asm.ca.gov
Palm Desert

Scott Baugh (R-67)
Term Limit: 2000
Huntington Beach

Tom J. Bordonaro Jr. (R-33)
Term Limit: 2000
tom.j.bordonaro@assembly.ca.gov
San Luis Obispo

Debra Bowen (D-53)
Term Limit: 1998
bowen@assembly.ca.gov
Torrance

Larry Bowler (R-10)
Term Limit: 1998
bowlerlw@assembly.ca.gov
Sacramento

Marilyn C. Brewer (R-70)
Term Limit: 2000
a70@assembly.ca.gov
Irvine

Valerie Brown (D-7)
Term Limit: 1998
valerie.brown@assembly.ca.gov
Santa Rosa

Cruz M. Bustamante (D-31)
Term Limit: 1998
cruz.bustamante@asm.ca.gov
Fresno

Bill Campbell (R-71)
Term Limit: 2002
bill.campbell@assembly.ca.gov
Orange

Tony Cardenas (D-39)
Term Limit: 2002
a39@assembly.ca.gov
Panorama City

Dennis A. Cardoza (D-26)
Term Limit: 2002
Turlock

Gil Cedillo (D-46)
Term Limit: 2004
Los Angeles

Jim Cunneen (R-24)
Term Limit: 2000
jim.cunneen@assembly.ca.gov
Campbell

Susan A. Davis (D-76)
Term Limit: 2000
davissa@assembly.ca.gov
San Diego

Denise Moreno Ducheny (D-79)
Term Limit: 2000
denise.ducheny@asm.ca.gov
National City

Martha M. Escutia (D-50)
Term Limit: 1998
martha.escutia@assembly.ca.gov
Huntington Park

Liz Figueroa (D-20)
Term Limit: 2000
liz.figueroa@assembly.ca.gov
Fremont

Brooks Firestone (R-35)
Term Limit: 2000
firestba@assembly.ca.gov
Santa Barbara

Richard Floyd (D-55)
Term Limit: 2000
Carson

Peter Frusetta (R-28)
Term Limit: 2000
peter.frusetta@assembly.ca.gov
Hollister

Martin Gallegos (D-57)
Term Limit: 2000
martin.gallegos@assembly.ca.gov
Irwindale

Jan Goldsmith (R-75)
Term Limit: 1998
jan.goldsmith@assembly.ca.gov
Poway

Brett Granlund (R-65)
Term Limit: 2000
brett.granlund@assembly.ca.gov
Yucaipa

Sally Havice (D-56)
Term Limit: 2002
sally.havice@assembly.ca.gov
Artesia

Robert M. Hertzberg (D-40)
Term Limit: 2002
hertzbrm@asm.ca.gov
Van Nuys

Mike Honda (D-23)
Term Limit: 2002
hondamm@asm.ca.gov
San Jose

George House (R-25)
Term Limit: 2000
george.house@assembly.ca.gov
Modesto

Howard Kaloogian (R-74)
Term Limit: 2000
howard.kaloogian@assembly.ca.gov
Carlsbad

Fred Keeley (D-27)
Term Limit: 2002
fred.keeley@asm.ca.gov
Santa Cruz

Wally Knox (D-42)
Term Limit: 2000
knoxwb@asm.ca.gov
Los Angeles

Sheila Kuehl (D-41)
Term Limit: 2000
Encino

Steven I. Kuykendall (R-54)
Term Limit: 2000
kuykenst@asm.ca.gov
Long Beach

Lynne C. Leach (R-15)
Term Limit: 2002
lynne.leach@asm.ca.gov
Walnut Creek

Ted Lempert (D-21)
Term Limit: 2000
ted.lempert@assembly.ca.gov
Palo Alto

Bill Leonard (R-63)
Term Limit: 2002
assemblyman.leonard@assembly.ca.
     gov
Rancho Cucamonga

Michael J. Machado (D-17)
Term Limit: 2000
mike.machado@asm.ca.gov
Stockton

Bob Margett (R-59)
Term Limit: 2000
a59@assembly.ca.gov
Arcadia

Diane Martinez (D-49)
Term Limit: 1998
diane.martinez@asm.ca.gov
Alhambra

Kerry Mazzoni (D-6)
Term Limit: 2000
kerry.mazzoni@assembly.ca.gov
San Rafael

Tom McClintock (R-38)
Term Limit: 2000
tom.mcclintock@assembly.ca.gov
Granada Hills

Carole Migden (D-13)
Term Limit: 2002
carole.migden@assembly.ca.gov
San Francisco

Gary Miller (R-60)
Term Limit: 2000
millergg@asm.ca.gov
City of Industry

Jim Morrissey (R-69)
Term Limit: 2000
a69@assembly.ca.gov
Santa Ana

Bill Morrow (R-73)
Term Limit: 1998
a73@assembly.ca.gov
Oceanside

Kevin Murray (D-47)
Term Limit: 2000
kevin.murray@assembly.ca.gov
Culver City

Grace F. Napolitano (D-58)
Term Limit: 1998
grace.napolitano@assembly.ca.gov
Santa Fe Springs

Keith Olberg (R-34)
Term Limit: 2000
keith.olberg@asm.ca.gov
Victorville

Thomas "Rico" Oller (R-4)
Term Limit: 2002
a04@assembly.ca.gov
Roseville

Deborah V. Ortiz (D-9)
Term Limit: 2002
a09@assembly.ca.gov
Sacramento

Rod Pacheco (R-64)
Term Limit: 2002
a64@assembly.ca.gov
Riverside

Lou Papan (D-19)
Term Limit: 2002
a19@assembly.ca.gov
Millbrae

Don Perata (D-16)
Term Limit: 2002
don.perata@assembly.ca.gov
Oakland

Charles S. Poochigian (R-29)
Term Limit: 2000
Fresno

Robert Prenter (R-30)
Term Limit: 2002
a30@assembly.ca.gov
Hanford

Curt Pringle (R-68)
Term Limit: 1998
curt.pringle@asm.ca.gov
Garden Grove

Bernie Richter (R-3)
Term Limit: 1998
Chico

George Runner (R-36)
Term Limit: 2002
a36@assembly.ca.gov
Lancaster

Jack Scott (D-44)
Term Limit: 2002
jack.scott@assembly.ca.gov
Pasadena

Kevin Shelley (D-12)
Term Limit: 2002
kevin.shelley@assembly.ca.gov
San Francisco

Virginia Strom-Martin (D-1)
Term Limit: 2002
a01@assembly.ca.gov
Santa Rosa

Michael Sweeney (D-18)
Term Limit: 2000
michael.sweeney@assembly.ca.gov
Hayward

Nao Takasugi (R-37)
Term Limit: 1998
Camarillo

Bruce Thompson (R-66)
Term Limit: 2000
a66@assembly.ca.gov
Temecula

Helen Thomson (D-8)
Term Limit: 2002
helen.thomson@assembly.ca.gov
Vacaville

Tom Torlakson (D-11)
Term Limit: 2002
tom.torlakson@assembly.ca.gov
Martinez

Antonio R. Villaraigosa (D-45)
Term Limit: 2000
antonio.villaraigosa@assembly.ca.gov
Los Angeles

Edward Vincent (D-51)
Term Limit: 2002
vincened@assembly.ca.gov
Ingelwood

Carl Washington (D-52)
Term Limit: 2002
Compton

Howard Wayne (D-78)
Term Limit: 2002
howard.wayne@assembly.ca.gov
San Diego

Scott Wildman (D-43)
Term Limit: 2002
a43@assembly.ca.gov
Glendale

Tom Woods Jr. (R-2)
Term Limit: 2000
tom.woods@assembly.ca.gov
Redding

Roderick Wright (D-48)
Term Limit: 2002
wrightrd@asm.ca.gov
Los Angeles

Useful Web Sites

California State Home Page:
http://www.ca.gov

California State Senate:
http://www.senate.ca.gov

California State Assembly:
http://www.assembly.ca.gov

California Geographical Survey:
http://goegodata.csun.edu/

California Higher Education Policy
     Center:
http://www.policycenter.org

Center for California Studies:
http://www.csus.edu/calst/index.html

California Voter Foundation:
http://www.calvoter.org

California government agency and
     commission list:
http://www.ganymede.org/
     agencies.html

University of California system:
http://www.ca.gov/s/learning/uc.html

California State University system:
http://www.ca.gov/s/learning/csu.html

California Historical Society:
http://www.calhist.org

California Court system:
http://www.courtinfo.ca.gov

California law references:
http://www.leginfo.ca.gov/calaw.html

Search bills in the California
     legislature:
http://www.sen.ca.gov/www/leginfo/
     SearchText.html

Southern California Association of
     Governments (SCAG):
http://www.scag.ca.gov

Association of Bay Area Governments
     (ABAG):
http://www.abag.ca.gov

Glossary

Absentee ballots Ballots not cast at a regular polling place.

Acculturate The process by which immigrants learn their new culture's language, customs, and traditions.

Amend To change a document such as a bill.

Appropriations Monies set aside for particular purposes.

Assimilation The process by which a new group learns the rules of the more established group and adopts its customs.

At-large election In contrast to a *district election*, a method of electing members of a city council or other legislative body by voters in the entire governmental unit.

Ballot initiative See *Initiative*.

Ballot status Appearing on the ballot, such as a political party.

Baseline budget A budget based on the previous year's budget. In contrast, a "zero-based" budget requires all programs to justify their existence.

Blanket primary A primary in which all candidates from every party are listed together.

Bond issues Interest-bearing government securities, authorized at the state or local level by voter approval of a ballot proposition, by which money is borrowed for prison construction or some other purpose.

Caucuses Groups organized to promote special causes.

Challenger In politics, a person who runs against an incumbent.

Civil liberties Protected types of behavior such as freedom of speech or religion, which governments are prohibited from taking away.

Civil rights Legally imposed obligations, such as the right to equal protection under the law or reasonable bail, that governments owe to individuals.

Civil service system A set of procedures for hiring government employees on the basis of merit, usually demonstrated by examination, and protecting them against unjust firing.

Class gap An increasing gap in resources between the wealthiest and the poorest people.

Closed primary The kind of primary election formerly used in California, in which only voters registered as members of a political party can vote for the nomination (selection) of that party's candidates. See also *Blanket primary.*

Conference committee A temporary committee appointed to resolve differences between the Senate and Assembly versions of a bill.

Conservative A political philosophy that favors smaller government, lower taxes, fewer public services, and a laissez-faire ("Let them do as they please") approach to business.

Constitutional offices The executive officials that the state constitution requires be elected by the voters.

Council-manager A form of city government in which the elected city council, with legislative authority, appoints, and can fire, a city manager to whom the various executive departments are responsible.

County committee Also known as *county central committee*; a group of elected party activists within each county.

Decline to state A voter's registration status when he or she does not wish to affiliate with any political party.

Deindustrialization Loss of industries and thus jobs, often seen as the results of automation, computerization, and the ability of capital to move anywhere labor is cheaper and profits are higher.

Demilitarization A reduction in military and defense-related industries with resulting losses in jobs.

Demographic shift Noticeable changes in population data, including numbers of people, size of ethnic groups, and so forth.

Devolution The passing of authority from federal to state and local governments.

Direct democracy The reforms of the Progressive movement, which enable voters to directly make laws, amend the state constitution, recall officials, or repeal laws passed by elected representatives.

District election An election in which a city, school district, or other government unit is divided into geographic districts, each of which has a representative elected by the voters in that district. See also *At-large election*.

Electoral votes The number of votes a state may cast in electing the President and Vice-President, computed by adding the number of its U.S. senators (2) to the number of representatives (52 for California as of 1990).

Electorate Those who vote.

Executive clemency The governor's power to lighten criminal sentences imposed by the courts by pardons, which cancel them; commutations, which reduce them; or reprieves, which postpone them. Amnesties are pardons for an entire group.

Ex officio Serving on a government body by virtue of holding an office.

Federalism A political arrangement in which the national and state systems have some powers independent of each other.

Felonies The most serious crimes, including murder, rape, and arson. See also *Misdemeanors*.

Franchise In politics, the right to vote.

Gerrymandering Drawing the boundaries of voting districts in order to favor the election of a particular group, individual, or candidate of the dominant political party.

Globalization Increasing spread of international trade and finance.

Grassroots Pertaining to actions, movements or organizations of a political nature that rely chiefly on the mass involvement of ordinary citizens.

Gubernatorial Pertaining to the office of governor.

Homophobia Fear and/or hatred of homosexuals.

Image making Creating a positive impression about a candidate through the use of public relations methods and mass media.

Immigrant-bashing The blaming of immigrants, whether legal or undocumented, for social problems.

Incumbent Person currently in office.

Indictment   Formal accusation of criminal behavior by a grand jury, sometimes used to bring defendants to trial.

Inferior courts   In California, the justice, municipal, and superior courts in which trials take place and whose judges are chosen differently than those on the courts of appeal and Supreme Court.

Infractions   Minor criminal offenses, such as jaywalking.

Initiative   The process by which citizens can propose a state or local law or amendment to the state constitution by signing a formal petition asking that it be submitted as a ballot proposition for voter approval.

Issue-oriented organizations   Groups concerned primarily with political issues, such as abortion, civil rights, and medical care, as opposed to groups interested in electing specific candidates.

Item veto   Sometimes called the *line-item veto*. The authority of the governor to reduce or eliminate money appropriated by the legislature for a specific purpose while signing the remaining provisions of the bill into law.

LAFCO   Local Agency Formation Commission.

Left-wing   A political approach that tends to value social equality and government intervention to achieve it rather than laissez-faire ("Let them do as they please").

Liberal   A political philosophy that supports active government involvement in creating a more just society and supports individual freedoms in personal matters.

Lobbying   The attempt to influence government policy, usually on behalf of an interest group.

Majority   More than 50 percent.

Mandates   Requirements; a federal mandate may require states to take a particular action.

Manifest Destiny   The justification of U.S. territorial expansion based on the mystical assumption that it was the clear fate of the nation to acquire at least all the land between the Atlantic and Pacific oceans.

Marginal   Uncertain, on the edge; a district, in contrast to the more numerous "safe" ones, in which the election outcome is uncertain because neither party has an overwhelming advantage in registered voters. See also *Safe district.*

Mayor-council   The traditional form of city government based on a separation of powers between a mayor with executive authority and a council with legislative authority, both elected by the voters.

Mestizo   Of mixed race, particularly Spanish European and pre-Columbian Indian heritage.

Minimalist   Limited to the simplest or most essential elements; politically, the usually conservative belief that government should do very little.

Misdemeanors   An intermediate level of crime, less damaging to persons or property than a *felony.*

Monocultural electorate   A term that describes the trend toward a largely white electorate in contrast with a largely nonwhite population.

Naturalization   The process of becoming a U.S. citizen.

Nonpartisan   Elections (such as those for judges, school board members, and city and county officials in California) in which the party affiliation of the candidates does not appear on the ballot.

Office-block ballot   To discourage straight-ticket party voting, the arrangement of candidates' names according to the office for which they are running rather than their party affiliation.

Open primary   See *Blanket primary.*

Ordinance   A law passed by a city or county.

Outmigration   The movement of people out of an area.

Out of the closet   A gay male or lesbian who is open about his or her sexual orientation.

Override   The process by which the legislative body votes again on a bill vetoed by the executive and overcomes the veto by a two-thirds majority so that the bill becomes law without the executive's approval.

Partisan   Any action or attitude reflecting strong loyalty to a party or political faction; in partisan elections, such as those of national and most state officials, the party affiliation of the candidates appears on the ballot.

Party affiliation   An individual's choice of a party when registering to vote; may or may not include any activity in that party.

Patronage   An elected official rewards supporters by granting them jobs.

Plaintiff   The person bringing suit in a civil case.

Plea bargain   Negotiations in a criminal case designed to get the defendant to plead guilty if the prosecution reduces the seriousness of the charge or reduces the sentence.

Plurality   The most votes.

Polarization   A sharp division between groups; for example, the increasing differences in views between conservative Republicans and liberal Democrats.

Political action committee (PAC)   An organization, usually formed by an interest group or corporation, designed to solicit money from individuals to be used for campaign contributions to candidates endorsed by the group.

Polls   Places where votes are cast.

President pro tem   The leader of the state Senate, elected by the membership.

Pressure groups   Organizations that lobby politicians to achieve their political and economic aims. Also known as *special interest groups.*

Private sector   Refers to all business and other activities that are not sponsored directly by government; however, much of the American private sector is subsidized through government funds.

Privatization   Any effort to cut back government and substitute private sector activity; for example, firing public janitors and "contracting out" to a private profit-seeking janitorial service.

Progressive movement   The growing demand in the early part of the century for such democratic reforms as the initiative and referendum.

Propositions   Items on the ballot that require a "yes" or "no" vote, including initiatives, referenda, recalls, and bond issues.

Public sector   Those activities and agencies sponsored by government and paid for from tax revenues.

Recall   A Progressive reform permitting the voters, by petition, to call a special election to remove an official from office before the next regularly scheduled election.

Recession   A period during which the economy slows down, leading to fewer jobs, higher unemployment, lower consumption, and reduced tax revenues.

Redistricting   Redrawing the boundaries of election districts; required after each census to keep district populations as nearly equal as possible.

Referendum   A type of ballot proposition that allows voters to repeal or revoke laws passed by the legislature.

Regressive   In reference to taxation, indicates that the poor are taxed more than the rich in proportion to their incomes.

Representative democracy   A system in which citizens cast their votes for representatives who will vote on the actual issues.

Runoff election   An election held when no candidate in a nonpartisan primary receives a majority; the two top candidates enter the "runoff" so that the final winner is elected by a majority vote.

Safe district   An election district in which one party, through *Gerrymandering,* is nearly guaranteed victory at the polls. See also *Marginal.*

Scapegoating   The process of blaming a social or ethnic group for society's problems.

Secession   Withdrawing from a political body.

Service economy   An economy dominated by service industries such as banking and health care.

Speaker of the Assembly   The presiding officer and most powerful member of the Assembly, elected by the membership.

Special districts   Local units of government that perform a service that no city or county provides, and which may encompass an area larger than any one city or county. Such districts have their own governing body, either appointed or elected.

Standing committees   Permanent committees of the California Senate and Assembly organized around policy subjects, to which every bill is referred and in which most of the work of legislation occurs.

States' rights   The concept that the fifty states must have autonomy in relation to the federal government.

Statutes   Laws that are in government code books and are not part of an actual constitution or charter.

Swing voters   Describes those whose votes are not predictable and who can be swayed to support candidates or issues. Also called *swing votes.*

Target audience   A select group of voters who receive political mailings with messages aimed at winning their support.

Tax assessment   In reference to property taxes, the amount that must be paid; it is based on the property's assessed value.

Two-tier society   A society that includes a small, affluent upper class; a large class of impoverished people (the working poor and the *underclass*); and a small middle class.

Underclass   Impoverished persons who survive through government assistance, charity, or criminal activity. They should not be confused with the "working poor," although income levels may be similar.

Unincorporated areas   Territory outside the boundaries of incorporated cities, whose residents receive nearly all municipal services from county government.

Unitary system   In contrast to a federal system, one in which the county and other regional or local governments have only the powers the state gives to them.

Upset   An election in which the outcome is a surprise to political observers.

User fees   Fees charged for recreational facilities and other public services so that those who use the services pay at least part of their costs.

Veto   The return of a bill unsigned by the chief executive to the legislative body that passed it. This "kills" the bill unless the legislature overrides the veto.

Bibliography

California Constitution Revision Commission, *Final Report and Recommendations to the Governor and Legislature* (Sacramento: Forum on Government Reform, 1996).

California Journal Roster/Government Guide (Sacramento: State Net, 1997).

Chan, Sucheng, and Spencer Olin, *Major Problems in California History* (Boston: Houghton Mifflin, 1997).

Clarke, Thurston, *California Fault: Searching for the Spirit of a State Along the San Andreas* (New York: Ballantine, 1996).

DeLeon, Richard, *Left Coast City: Progressive Politics in San Francisco, 1975–1991* (Lawrence: University Press of Kansas, 1991).

Fay, James S., and Ronald J. Boehm, eds., *California Almanac 1993* (Santa Barbara: Pacific Data Resources, 1993).

Hohm, Charles F., *California's Social Problems* (New York: Longman, 1997).

King, Rob, M. Poster, and S. Olin, *Postsuburban California: The Transformation of Orange County Since World War II* (Berkeley: University of California Press, 1991).

Lamare, James W., *California Politics: Economics, Power, and Policy* (Minneapolis/St. Paul: West Books, 1994).

League of Women Voters of California, *A Guide to California Politics* (Sacramento, 1992).

Lembke, Bud, and Larry Lynch, *Political Pulse* (Sacramento: Lembke and Lynch, 1997).

McWilliams, Carey, *North from Mexico: The Spanish-Speaking People of the United States* (New York: Greenwood Press, 1968).

Rodriguez, Richard, *Days of Obligation: An Argument with My Mexican Father* (New York: Viking, 1992).

Rosengarten, Dick, *California Political Week* (Beverly Hills: Calpeek, 1997).

Starr, Kevin, *Inventing the Dream* (New York: Oxford University Press, 1985).

U.S. Department of Commerce, Bureau of the Census, *Statistical Abstract of the United States, 1993.*

Wilson, E. Dotson, *California's Legislature* (Sacramento: Office of the Chief Clerk, California State Assembly, 1994).

Index